Covenant and Calling

*Towards a Theology
of Same-Sex Relationships*

Robert Song

scm press

© Robert Song 2014

Published in 2014 by SCM Press
Editorial office
3rd Floor
Invicta House
108–114 Golden Lane
London
EC1Y OTG

SCM Press is an imprint of Hymns Ancient & Modern Ltd
(a registered charity)
13A Hellesdon Park Road
Norwich
NR6 5DR, UK

www.scmpress.co.uk

British Library Cataloguing in Publication data

A catalogue record for this book is available
from the British Library

978 0 334 05188 6

Typeset by Manila Typesetting
Printed and bound by
CPI Group (UK) Ltd, Croydon

In memory of
Michael Vasey
(1946–98)
'Jerusalem the Golden'

Contents

Acknowledgements

My first debt of gratitude is to Joe Pilling, who chaired the Church of England House of Bishops Working Group on Human Sexuality, and whose kind invitation to me to join the working group as an adviser provided the context in which the thoughts in this book germinated. The group's discussions were intense and demanding, but also very rewarding, and I am thankful to him, and to all those in the group for their warmth and collegiality: Jonathan Baker, Malcolm Brown, Martin Davie, Jessica Martin, Michael Perham, Keith Sinclair, John Stroyan, and Rachel Treweek; as well as those around the country who openly and generously shared their experience with us.

The ideas in this book were aired at seminars given in Durham and Aberdeen, and I am grateful to those who participated in them, as well as to the following for the kind of insights that arise only in conversation: David Atkinson, Stephen Barton, Vicky Beeching, Dorothee Bertschmann, Nigel Biggar, Brian Brock, Joe Cassidy, Conor Cunningham, Andrew Goddard, Gerard Loughlin, Margaret Masson, Mike Mawson, John Milbank, Walter Moberly, Oliver O'Donovan, Anna Poulson, Gene Rogers, Helen Savage, Peter Selby, Maeve Sherlock, Harry Smart, Iona Song, Stuart Weeks, and Philip Wheatley. As ever, conversation implies not agreement, but a willingness to engage.

I am particularly grateful to John Barclay, who encouraged me to turn my early thoughts into a book, and to him and several others who very kindly read through and commented on a draft of the text: Stephen Barton, Nicolas Baumgartner, Robert MacSwain, Margaret Masson, Maeve Sherlock and Catherine Wilcox.

Two friends deserve special mention: Mark Hearne, whose chance comment over a quarter of a century ago opened a door that has never closed; and Michael Vasey, who was by turns brilliant and exasperating, and who taught me much of what I know about living with these questions. And to my wife Margaret, and children Iona and Jamie, for all their love and care, as ever, and in particular for their tolerance and patience beyond anything I could have reasonably asked, even as I rushed to finish a book on a subject about which I once vowed I would never write.

Preface

This is not the first book on the subject of theology and sexual relationships, and short of an asteroid incinerating the biosphere or the Lord returning in a way more spectacular than Anglicans are used to expecting, it will not be the last. It is written at a time widely thought to be one of crisis for the churches, a time when they are persistently threatened by the prospect of schism over matters of sexuality, but when renewed efforts are also being made to defuse tensions by calling on participants on all sides to lay down arms and enter into talks.

My aim is to make a contribution to these conversations, not by providing a detached overview of the issues, but by seeking to explore what potential there might be for taking the discussion forward, in a way that is both fully responsive to the tradition of Christian teaching and liturgical practice, and yet willing to entertain the possibility that we still have more to learn. In particular, I want to ask not so much about sexuality as about the relationships within which sexuality is expressed. Historically the churches have recognized two vocations, marriage and celibacy. Marriage has been understood as the lifelong and exclusive commitment to one another of a man and a woman, the only appropriate context for sexual relationship. Celibacy – or at least sexual abstinence – has been regarded as the proper and only legitimate alternative. The question I want to investigate is whether these really represent the sole alternatives, or whether we could draw from within the terms of the tradition the lineaments of another, third vocation. Might it be possible to conceive of another kind of calling, one that arises out of the heart not only of Christian understandings of marriage and celibacy, but also of what these tell us about our created, bodily natures and our hope in Christ?

There has of course been no shortage of defences of same-sex relationships, appealing to models of lesbian or gay friendship, of quasi-marital same-sex union, or of equal marriage, from which there is a great deal to learn. But many of them convey a sense of not having really done full justice to the thick texture of Christian thinking about sexuality. This is not so much a matter of how they handle scriptural texts in the area – though that remains a standing question – as a failure to deal adequately with the fact that fundamental to Christian understandings of marriage throughout the centuries has been the assumption that it is a *creation* good, and consequently intrinsically open to procreation. The other goods and virtues of marriage, such as its commitments to faithfulness and permanence, are frequently assumed to be separable in principle from procreativity, but without a really compelling theological justification. The rich Christian narrative of creation and redemption, which I will argue might provide a fuller theological rationale and point the way to such a separation, never properly comes into view.

Interestingly, a parallel kind of failure to place ourselves within the Christian theological narrative can be discerned behind many more conservative accounts of marriage and sexuality. While they may claim, and not without cause, to be closer to the surface meaning of many pertinent biblical texts, and may also rightly sustain the sense of marriage as a created good, they frequently forget that according to the Christian narrative of the redemption of the world in Christ the Church has no ultimate stake in the propagation of the species or the indefinite continuation of society outside of Christ. The survival of the human species and the perpetuation of this world order are not independent goods to which Christians whose identity is rooted in the resurrection have to pay obeisance, but are themselves relativized by Christ, who alone is the substance of Christian hope. And this cannot but affect our understanding of sexuality.

In both cases the decisive failure is one of not recognizing the significance of the advent of Christ for sexuality. Sex BC is not the same as sex AD. Before Christ, marriage as a good of creation was inseparable from procreation; but after Christ, while marriage and procreation do not stop being goods, we are also directed to a future resurrection life in which marriage and procreation will be no more. The vocation of celibacy is the first sign of this resurrection life, witnessing as it does to a time when God will be known as the fulfilment of all our desires. The question is whether this 'time between the times' in which we live, between Christ's resurrection and his return in glory, also admits of another calling. Is there space for another kind of vocational structure, a structure of relationship, which might also be an appropriate way of inhabiting this theological time between the times? Could such a relationship be sexually expressed? And what would sexuality signify in such circumstances?

In the chapters that follow, I will explore the arguments for such a third vocation, which I will call 'covenant partnership'. The decisive feature that distinguishes this proposal from many other similar defences of same-sex partnerships is that it is rooted in the eschatological character of the time we indwell, that is, the time when in Christ the ultimate destiny of the creation has been revealed, but when it has yet to be fulfilled in our experience. A result of this, so I shall argue, is that covenant partnerships would in principle include not only same-sex relationships and relationships involving transsexuals or people with intersex conditions, but also opposite-sex relationships. One of the assumptions that tends to stand unquestioned is that the primary theological problem with same-sex sexual relationships is that they are same-sex. I argue by contrast that the fundamental division is not between heterosexual and homosexual relationships, but between procreative and non-procreative relationships. Covenant partnerships are different from the created good of procreative marriage precisely because they are not procreative: by which is meant not that they could never involve bringing up children, but that children would not be the direct result of the couple's sexual relationship. Whether and under what circumstances covenant partnerships might involve the nurturing and raising of children involves a wide range of considerations, which I do not address in this book.

In exploring the case for covenant partnerships, there are three paths I have tried not to follow. First, although the book reaches towards conclusions that differ from those that historic Christianity has generally arrived at, it is not programmatically 'liberal'. I do not take as axiomatic certain methodological approaches or normative commitments that are typically associated with more liberal or radical styles of theology. I do not for example argue for a principled methodological privileging of experience over Scripture, tradition or reason, nor do I interpret reason as a realm of self-grounded truth standing autonomously over against Scripture or tradition. One of the many results of the current predicament over gender and sexuality within the churches has been what can only be described as an increasing fear of Scripture in some quarters, and a consequent anxiety about teaching, preaching or learning from it – a situation that over time could become debilitating for Christian witness. If the Christian Church has anything to say to the world at all, it must be grounded in what it has learned of God through Jesus Christ; and what it knows of Jesus Christ it knows in the first place by attending to the witness of the apostles who proclaimed him and the prophets who foretold him. Subsequent church tradition – in the form of the canons, creeds and councils of official teaching, or in the writings of theologians, ecclesiastical, learned or lay – gains its authority to the extent that it is able to be illuminated by, and therefore in response to shed light on, that primary witness and the one to whom it points. And this cannot but make central the work of seeking to understand Scripture.

Of course, if we learn of Jesus Christ by attention to the preaching of the apostles and the words of the prophets, it does not follow that the task of theology and theological ethics is the simple reiteration of what they said. For the Church now, the question is not merely an antiquarian enterprise of uncovering the meanings of ancient texts, but rather the properly theological venture of discerning their meaning for us in our world. As Karl Barth declared, Christian theology as such 'does not ask what the apostles and prophets said but what we must say on the basis of the apostles and prophets'.[1] We cannot assume that faithfulness consists in the bald repetition of what has been said in the past; to say the same

---

1 Karl Barth, *Church Dogmatics* I/1 [1936], trans. G. W. Bromiley, second edition, Edinburgh: T. & T. Clark, 1975, p. 16.

word in a different context is to say a different word. Revelation is properly speaking an event in which the living God speaks, not a deposit which we can regard as safely tied up because we hold to a high view of biblical authority or because we proclaim our faithfulness to the received tradition. We are not in a position to control how God may choose to speak, and our incompetence in this is not eased by efforts to lay down a hermeneutical method in advance, or to parade our agreement with previous generations of church teachers. Rather our responsibility is always one of exercising judgement, learning how we are to think and act now, in the knowledge that our thinking and acting are finally made right not because of the correctness of our judgements, but because we ourselves live under the mercy of God's judgement. Undoubtedly we should seek to think and to act on the basis of our best understandings of the sources of authority, but the Word of God always exceeds these. If we will be saved finally, it will not be because we are faithful to our understanding of the Bible or the tradition, but because God is faithful to us.

One corollary of this understanding of theology is a wariness of importing too readily the preferred idioms and conceptualities of contemporary secular culture. The vocabulary of rights, to take one example, is often deployed as a lever to prise open an entrance for habits of thought that require at the very least considerable scrutiny: talk of 'my right to sexual self-expression' is not likely to be the language of choice for those who have come to know that they have been bought with a price, and that their body is not their own (1 Cor. 6.19–20). Certainly the demand for respect for people's human rights does bring to life important aspects of moral truth for us now, and powerful and effective appeals to the language of rights have often been made to draw attention to injustice, not least in the wake of the magnificent international declarations of rights that followed the Second World War. But even if rights-talk is something that Christian theology may properly wish to endorse in particular circumstances, there is also a strong case for thinking that it should not be its primary moral language. It too easily suggests a vision of society as constituted by self-sufficient individuals who contract to enter into social relationships only when it suits their interests, and who fail to recognize that from before the day they are born they are embedded in a network of relationships which sustain them and which in turn they are called to sustain. Of itself it has too impoverished an understanding of human beings to provide an adequate rendering of the Christian moral vision.

The second path I have attempted not to take is to accede to suggestions that change in moral teaching should be driven by demands that the Church move with the times, or that it should change its ethical norms to fit perceived missiological needs. To be sure, exceptionally insistent pastoral problems are raised for the churches in most Western countries by their historic teaching on sexuality. The churches now give the impression to many among their increasing ranks of despisers to be not just the bearers of different cultural practices, which might be defended by appeal to legitimate religious difference, but to be positively immoral, their perceived rejection of gays and lesbians in effect acting as a kind of anti-witness. It is a position of considerable peril for the mission of the churches, needless to say, when one of the first things people associate with them is hatred of gays and other sexual minorities.

Yet even so, this is a time for discernment, and not for panic. The way in which contemporary Western cultures think about and perform sexuality has itself become far too distorted for us blithely to assume that simply signing up and joining in could clear up the churches' remaining problems. Sexuality pursued in a consumerist mode, which all too easily becomes sexuality that is pornographic, predatory or promiscuous, is not the finest basis from which to launch a defence of Western values. To raise questions about it, a lot that appears to have fallen to the churches, may not be quite the act of betrayal that it is often portrayed as being. The churches have a lot of work to do themselves in relation to sexuality, as no one needs to remind them, but they are not the only ones who face profound self-questioning.

A third path frequently trodden which I have sought to avoid raises a concern that may initially appear more esoteric, but is in fact of crucial theological significance. In one way or another, many theological defences of same-sex relationships seek to play down the created nature of bodies and bodily difference, and as a result they arguably run the danger of being incipiently 'docetic' in nature. The ancient heresy of docetism centred on the claim that the earthly body of Jesus was apparent rather than real. Such an idea may have proved attractive to some of those who wanted to secure the truth that God transcends the material creation that is subject to change and decay, but it was rejected from very early on, on the grounds that it suggested the denial of the goodness of creation and of the salvation of human beings through Christ's redemptive identification with their bodily nature. 'By this you know the Spirit of God,' the first epistle of John declares, 'every spirit that confesses that Jesus Christ has come in the flesh is from God' (1 John 4.2). In terms of theological anthropology, this obliges us to question any understanding of human beings that in effect portrays the flesh as the external and contingent clothing of the 'real me', and sees the true self as fleshless spirit.

Of course, those who defend same-sex relationships in a way that may be susceptible to such criticism do not deny that human beings are made of flesh, nor do they say that bodies are bad. On the contrary, for them the body is celebrated as a source of good – bodies, particular bodies, evoke desire and delight, and in so doing direct us to the God who is the origin and goal of all true desire. However, when it is asserted or implied that one's sex is immaterial, or that there is in principle no connection at all in creation between sex and procreation, we might begin to wonder whether we are beginning to witness the denial of our nature as body–soul unities. We may regard bodies as good, but our thought may still be tacitly dualistic; and as the Protestant ethicist Paul Ramsey observed, modern 'good-body' dualism is just as dualistic as ancient 'bad-body' dualism.[2] It is not enough to say that by contrast with ancient dualisms sex is regarded as a good in such modern accounts, and therefore that matter matters. An emphasis on relationality which sees one's sex as indifferent

---

2 Paul Ramsey, 'Sexuality in the History of Redemption', *Journal of Religious Ethics* 16:1 (1988), pp. 56–86 (p. 82, n. 3).

disregards the sexed nature of bodies that is *in some sense* given with creation – even if, as we shall see, the precise nature of this needs to be carefully thought through. If we are going to endorse same-sex relations in some way, we have to seek to do so in terms that do not evidently deny what the Christian tradition has wished to affirm about the goodness of creation and the humanity of Christ.

This is particularly a concern when one seeks to explore the significance of eschatology for sexual ethics, as I do. The language of an eschatological ethics of sex will raise in some minds the spectre of the libertarian visions of free love associated with millennarian movements down the ages, variously rejecting marriage, promoting unfettered sexual choice, and languidly grazing in the gardens of forbidden pleasure. Some versions of this may have been what Paul found to his alarm in the Corinthian church. However, nothing in the proposals put forward in this book legitimates a sexual free-for-all or the belief that it does not matter what Christians do with their bodies, readers may or may not be pleased to know. A gulf separates the idea that there is a vocation to covenant partnership, grounded in the teaching that there will be no marriage and therefore no procreation in heaven, from the idea that freedom in Christ is a licence to embark on distant voyages of unbounded sexual exploration. Eschatology may be the fulfilment of creation, but it is not its denial.

It is one thing to attempt to avoid more liberal styles of theological reasoning or secular patterns of thought or docetic mentalities, but quite another to have succeeded in doing so. Perhaps the greatest danger of enterprises like the present one is that of self-deception; it may be that it should be judged an exercise in rationalization, the legitimation of conclusions reached on entirely other grounds. Whether the present essay is finally susceptible to such a criticism is for the reader to decide; we each need the company and correction of others. This is especially salient for myself as a member of the Church of England: while shared, corporate discernment is important for all churches in all times and places, it has taken on a particular significance in recent times for Anglicans. For it has become perhaps the peculiarly Anglican vocation to seek to hold together strands of Christian identity that others have found it easier to separate, and to aspire to do so in a way that represents not just a politically secured *modus vivendi*, but itself forms a distinctive witness to the Church's promised unity in Christ. Just as contemporary Anglicans do not believe – even secretly – that one has to be an Anglican to be a true Christian, so they are a living embodiment of a sense of human frailty in the grasp of truth. And so conversation, communal discernment, and the effort to hear Christ in one another and under the authority of Scripture, tradition and reason have become the hallmark of Anglican ecclesiology at its best. This book is offered in that spirit.

I

The Beginning and End of Marriage

We could start our thinking about a theology of sexual relationships from any number of places. For example, we might begin by reflecting on the nature of desire – our desire for each other, our desire for God, and, grounding and sustaining these, God's desire for us. Or we might think about what it means to be embodied, not just angelic beings or pure intellects, but fleshly creatures who relate to one another in our physical presence. Or we might choose to reflect on our cultural context, pondering the meaning of the revolution in attitudes towards sex that has transformed Western society in the past half-century. All of these will have a place in any full theological account of sexuality, and I shall have something to say about all of them in the course of the following chapters.

But a very strong case can be made for beginning at the beginning, with the opening chapters of Genesis. Not only is it the place where the canonical Christian Bible starts, a fact itself of theological significance, it is also and even more importantly the place to which, at the heart of his teaching on the subject, Jesus himself points. If we are to understand how Christian theology thinks of sexuality and marriage, we need therefore to attend first to the Genesis passages and their portrayal of humankind as created in the image of God. Following that, we will be in a position to consider what it means to say that Christ is the fulfilment of creation, and therefore what it means for marriage to be fulfilled in Christ; this correspondingly will direct us towards the dramatic change that the advent of Christ opens up for the Christian understanding of sexuality.

Creation and the ends of marriage

'From the beginning of creation,' says Jesus according to the Gospel of Mark, '"God made them male and female". For this reason a man shall leave his father and mother and be joined to his wife, and the two shall become one flesh' (Mark 10.6–8).[1] In his words on marriage, Jesus draws into a unity two different strands of narrative in the first two chapters of Genesis, which conventional historical criticism has tended to attribute to separate original sources. The first, which centres on Genesis 1.26–28, sets the creation of human beings in the narrative of the seven days of creation. Following on from the creation of the creatures of the sea, the birds of the air, and the animals on the earth, God creates humankind, declaring that they are made in God's image, and that they are to have dominion over all the other creatures.

> [27]So God created humankind in his image,
>   in the image of God he created them;
>   male and female he created them.
> [28]God blessed them, and God said to them, 'Be fruitful and multiply, and fill the earth and subdue it; and have dominion over the fish of the sea and over the birds of the air and over every living thing that moves upon the earth.' (Gen. 1.27–28)

Being created in God's image is related, according to this passage, to being created male and female, which in turn is related closely to God's blessing and God's command to be fruitful, to fill the earth and subdue it. The second passage, in Genesis 2, describes the origins of the sexes rather differently. First, an original human being, *adam*, is formed out of the dust of the ground (*adamah*), given the breath of life, and placed in the garden of Eden to look after it. After permitting the *adam* to eat freely of any tree of the garden, except the tree of the knowledge of good and evil, God then declares: 'It is not good that the *adam* should be alone; I

---

1 All biblical quotations are taken from the New Revised Standard Version, unless otherwise indicated.

will make him a helper as his partner' (Gen. 2.18). In response to this need, God creates all the animals for the *adam* to name, but none of them are found to be adequate as a partner. Only at this point is the woman created from a rib taken out of the side of the *adam* while he sleeps; she is one whom he recognizes as bone of his bones and flesh of his flesh, one called Woman, for she is taken out of Man. And so the story leads to the conclusion referred to by Jesus, that therefore a man leaves his partner and clings to his wife, and they become one flesh (Gen. 2.24).

Much could be said about these passages, and I will return to them several times. For now I want to emphasize three themes which the Christian tradition has drawn from them in relation to marriage. First, Christian theology affirms that we are to understand marriage as a *created* good. To say that it is a created good is to say that it is not merely 'natural'. It is not just an empirical regularity: it is not something whose truth can be established – or indeed denied – on the basis of scientific observation, whether by anthropological or sociological or historical generalizations about human societies across time, or by zoological comparisons with other apparently lifelong pair-bonding species such as common ravens or prairie voles. The various human and natural sciences may have insights, no doubt of differing levels of profundity, into the ways in which marriage in its endless variations has been socially and culturally constructed, but from a theological perspective they do not exhaust the meaning of marriage; they cannot of themselves determine what marriage as a created ordinance *is*.

Second, marriage is a created *good*. That is, it is intended for and oriented to human flourishing. It is a gift of a good God which serves the good of the partners, of their children and wider family, and of society as a whole. It is not a necessary evil which is required in order to ward off even worse evils; if theologians in the Christian tradition have often cast marriage in an apparently negative light, for example seeing it as a remedy against sin, or have been unenthusiastic about it when compared with, say, celibacy, they have never thereby depicted it as an evil. On the contrary, their point has been precisely that its role is one of training in holiness, restraining the lusts that war against the soul. And at their best they have recognized that marriage, as the gift of a good God who is drawing all creation towards himself, can itself be a means by which we are taken up into the love of the Triune God.

Third, marriage in creation has a structure, of which we can isolate two decisive aspects. The first is that it is about the faithful and permanent relationship of the partners. Immediately after the declaration that God will make humankind in God's own image, and the connection of this with dominion over the other living creatures (1.26), God declares that they are made 'male and female', with an intrinsic mutual relationality. Man exists vis-à-vis woman, and woman exists vis-à-vis man. This aspect of relationality is brought out more explicitly in the second creation story. God's recognition that it is not good that the *adam* be alone is a declaration that solitary existence is not how human beings flourish: human beings are intrinsically social animals, as would be affirmed by later philosophers, and come to their fulfilment through the mutual support and companionship that is found in faithful, permanent relationship. Here in the second story we should also note that the fulfilment is related to a task: the partner is to be a helper in the task of tilling and keeping the garden, that is, of ensuring its fruitfulness.

The element of a shared task, of the fruitfulness of the relationship of Adam and Eve, is an indication in the Genesis narratives that marriage is not solely for the mutual satisfaction of the husband and wife. And this leads us to the second aspect of the structure of marriage in creation, namely that it has a specific orientation to having children. We can see this from the fact that the declaration that human beings are made male and female in Genesis 1.27 is immediately followed by God's pronouncement of blessing and God's command that they be fruitful and multiply in 1.28. Children do not appear here as an optional extra to the otherwise self-contained nature of marriage. They are not extrinsic or contingent, a lifestyle accessory to be added on should the happy couple decide this would make their happiness complete. Rather, as presented in Genesis, the procreation and nurture of children is an inseparable and intrinsic good of marriage, the result of God's

4

blessing and command to be fruitful. And such procreation and nurture arises out of the relationship of the man and the woman, not in independence from it. Children are not inserted into the partners' companionship from the outside by the wave of a wand, but are a blessing of God that arises from the heart of the relationship of male and female: a child is the entirely proper and fitting expression in the oneness of his or her flesh of the parents' own one-flesh bond.

There are other features of marriage that might be drawn out of these narratives. For example, the idea that the man leaves his mother and father may suggest that marriage requires a partner from outside the immediate family. Again, the fact that the passages speak solely of the relationship of the one man and the one woman has often been taken to imply that the marriage relationship and the family unit are the basis of society, the seedbed from which future citizens are nurtured, the cells of which the larger social organism is comprised, the bricks out of which the social edifice is built. And the taking of the woman from the man's side, as the generic, sexless *adam* seamlessly becomes the male Adam, has often been taken to legitimate the patriarchal ordering of society and the subordination of women – a conclusion that at any rate the second of the two Genesis narratives does rather little to disrupt.

However, I concentrate on the elements of mutual relationship and procreativity because those are the features that were emphasized in the classical Christian understanding of marriage. Ever since Augustine, the Christian tradition has talked of three 'goods' of marriage, three ends that jointly constitute marriage, that together distinguish marriage from all other forms of human relationship, and without any one of which marriage ceases to be marriage. For Augustine, whose reflections on marriage developed through repeated wrestling with these passages in Genesis, the goods of marriage came to be understood as one marital good, summed up in three words: *proles* (offspring), *fides* (faithfulness), and *sacramentum* (the bond of permanence).

The first of these, *proles*, initially occupied an uncertain place for Augustine; his earlier writings suggest an ambivalence whether there would have been procreation before the fall. Although he never followed some Eastern Christian speculations (such as those of Gregory of Nyssa) that originally human beings shared a primordial androgynous unity, and that the division of human beings into male and female was itself related to a fall from spiritual to material nature, it was initially unclear to him what need there might be for sexually differentiated organs. Only in his later writings, notably the *City of God*, when he had come to locate sin in the will rather than the body, did he unambiguously affirm the created goodness of biological materiality and sexual differentiation. The purpose of sexual differentiation he came to locate solely in procreation, and the goodness of bodily sexual difference was underlined in his emphasis that it would still be found in the new creation.

The second good of marriage, *fides*, is conceptualized by Augustine primarily in terms of the restraint of sexual sin. For him this is not just a matter of marriage providing a legitimate outlet for sexual desire, thereby reducing the temptation to infidelity and the consequent disruption to social and civic harmony. Marriage also remedies sexual desire itself: for Augustine, the sexual act involves the temporary loss of the body's proper subjection to the rational will, and since the subordination of the passions to reason is integral to human virtue, sex is therefore intrinsically morally problematic. Celibacy is always superior to marriage, and sex may only be redeemed by being oriented to the having of children (although Augustine does allow that a partner who submits to having sex in order to satisfy their partner's desire for it commits a pardonable sin!).

It is with the third good, the bond of permanence, that Augustine introduces a theme that goes decisively beyond the Genesis accounts. It is based on the connection made in Ephesians 5.32 between the marriage relationship and the relationship between Christ and the Church: that husband and wife become one flesh, the writer says, 'is a great mystery, and I am applying it to Christ and the church'. Not only is marriage a participation in the creation order found from the beginning from before the fall, it also performs a role witnessing to the new life that connects Christ to the Church. Marriage is not just grounded in an understanding of creation, but also in some way signifies God's relationship to

God's people. This reflects a theme found in the Old Testament (e.g. Jer. 2 — 3; Hos. 1 — 3), according to which God's relationship to Israel had often been portrayed as a marriage, one marked by frequent unfaithfulness on the part of Israel, but by constancy and faithfulness on the part of God. And it justifies the language of covenant in relation to marriage, that is, the public undertaking by the two partners of promises of committed faithfulness one to the other, together with the growth in relationship that emerges out of such commitments.

Augustine's account of the three goods was enormously influential on subsequent Christian teaching, even though it has been subject to substantial reinterpretation in accordance with later theological preoccupations. Different orderings and enumerations of the goods have been offered, and different accounts of what is meant by a good of marriage elaborated, some emphasizing what marriage is, others why couples might wish to enter upon it. For the sake of clarity, in this book I will regularly refer to faithfulness, permanence and procreation as the goods of marriage. By faithfulness, I mean not just the commitment of the partners to forsake all others and stay faithful to the marital bed, but also to provide mutual support, protection and love. By permanence is meant not an indissoluble, sacramental bond which makes divorce ontologically impossible, as found in Roman Catholic teaching, but the moral bond created by the promise of faithfulness so long as both partners shall live. By procreation I mean an openness to having children as the result of the couple's sexual relationship, mindful of the fact that not all marriages will in fact be fertile. These three do not sum up everything that there is to be said about marriage, but they do isolate the features that are relevant for my argument, for reasons that will become clear.

Christ and the fulfilment of creation

In the Christian tradition, therefore, we find an understanding of marriage as a created good, with a structure characterized by the ends of procreation and nurture of children, the faithfulness of the partners each to the other to the exclusion of all others, and the commitment to permanence until death. As a *good* of creation, it is instituted for human flourishing; as a good of *creation*, it is identified as a universal good, one whose nature can never be finally determined by human scientific understanding.

However, as is clear from the analogy in Ephesians between the relation of husband and wife and that of Christ and the Church, creation cannot be understood separately from its fulfilment in Christ. We need therefore to explore more fully the significance that the coming of Jesus Christ holds for the theology of marriage. Here the decisive thing we have to appreciate is that for Christian theology creation is not an independent realm, an autonomous structure of being with its own logic, to which Christ is then added as an afterthought or a supplement. The doctrine of creation is not a timeless theological truth which can be detached from its context in the story of God's dealings with all that is not God. As we have seen, this means on the one hand that creation cannot be understood as 'nature', a supposedly metaphysically complete and independent realm whose properties could be exhaustively analysed by the sciences. But it also means, on the other, that the doctrine of creation is theologically inseparable from an understanding of Christ. This is the force of the magnificent passage in the opening chapter of Colossians, in which Christ is described as the firstborn of all creation, the one through whom and for whom all things were made, who was before all things, and in whom all things hold together (Col. 1.15–18; cf 1 Cor. 8.6). Christ is the one who makes creation cohere, in virtue of whom creation is good and has meaning. And of course this idea is found supremely in the grand, rolling periods that open the Gospel of John: in the beginning was the Word, the Word who was with God, the Word who was God, the Word through whom all things came into being, without whom not one thing came into being (John 1.1–3). It is not that Genesis tells us how things are 'naturally' and that Christ provides later, additional information, but rather that all creation has its being aboriginally in Christ. To use a concept that Irenaeus of Lyons developed on the basis of Ephesians 1.9–10, Christ 'recapitulates' creation, gathering up in himself the entire history of created being, both human and non-human.

That creation may not be understood as mere 'nature' does not mean that there is no connection between creation and the structures and processes of the natural world, as if the theological concept of creation floated above the material world like a vaporous fog. The created world is not something other than the natural world; rather they are related in that through the workings of nature there can be discerned something of the glory of God and the nature of the good for human beings. In Romans 1.20 Paul declares that God's eternal power and divine nature can be known through the things God has made. And in Psalm 19 the heavens proclaim the glory of God, in voices without words yet full of speech, while by analogy the law of the Lord announces the Lord's decrees in words, rejoicing the heart and making wise the simple (Ps. 19.1–4, 7–10). The law of the Lord is oriented to the created good for humankind, and this gives some limited legitimation to the notion of natural law. And yet such legitimation must be carefully circumscribed. First, what we can learn from nature alone has been fatally compromised because, as Paul puts it, humanity has not honoured God or given thanks to him, and so they have become futile in their thinking (Rom. 1.21). As a result humankind is without excuse in the sight of God and will perish, both Gentiles who do not possess the Torah yet are able to learn by nature what the Torah requires, and Jews who have the Torah and so will be judged by the Torah (Rom. 2.12–16). We have enough knowledge to condemn us, but not enough to guide us to the truth and save us. Second, natural law may not be understood unevangelically, that is, without reference to Christ. Nature itself is graced: it is not a 'pure' nature that can be known by the operations of 'pure' philosophical reason as if God did not exist, but something that in the divine economy is always related to Christ who is the one in whom it coheres. Natural law is known in and through Christ who is its origin and fulfilment.

For theology, therefore, to talk of marriage as a good of creation is to indicate that it is not just to be understood in terms gleaned from Genesis in separation from an understanding of Christ as the fulfilment of creation and as its very basis. By referring marriage to the relationship of Christ and the Church, marriage is shown to embody and reflect the relationship of God to God's people. In turn this means that marriage is to be understood in terms of a covenant, the basic scriptural and theological category that defines that relationship, according to which God chooses to be the God of Israel, and in Christ to take as his covenant partner first Israel and then through the Church the whole of humankind, Gentiles and Jews alike; in which God's promise to be his people's God is met in return by their promise to be his people. And, in turn again, it may be that we can see this covenant relationship bearing witness to the inner life of the Trinitarian God. As God is in his external relations to the creation, so he is in his eternal relations within himself. As God creates not out of whim, nor out of necessity, but out of free love for his creation, so also the creation is the outworking of the eternal and free covenant commitment internal to the Godhead. In our finite covenant relationships, we bear witness to the eternal covenant relationships within the very being of God.

We should note the direction of the relationship between human and divine. It is not that marriage is the given, the epistemological starting point from which we may begin to understand something of the nature of God. And it is certainly not that human efforts at stable relationship are the reality, and the human relationship with God or the inner divine relationships a projection on to the sky that legitimates and stabilizes particular human social orders. Rather, human covenant commitments are a reflection of the divine covenant commitment to human beings, which in turn reflects God's inner Trinitarian relations. And human relationships bear witness to the prior divine relationship not as a mere illustration, a contingent and external likeness to the divine covenant commitment, but as themselves in some small part a participation in that divine covenant relationship. This participation of the human in the divine reality is not an identity of being: to name among the many obvious and fundamental differences, the love of God for God's people is not the love of one equal to another but of the Creator for the created; and the commitment of God to his people is irrevocable, whereas human commitments are inconstant and fickle. But nor is the human participation in the divine reality solely an agreement of name, as if human covenants were one thing and the divine covenant commitment something entirely different. Rather, the relationship is analogical: certain features of God's relationship to God's people are imaged in a married couple's relationship to each other, but not all.

This theological context is crucial for understanding marriage, since it finally makes intelligible why faithfulness and permanence are intrinsic to marriage. Marriage, to repeat, is a natural good, part of created human reality and oriented to human flourishing. But if that natural good is shorn of its theological context and left to float free, it readies itself to be understood naturalistically, in purely immanent terms. And understood in this way, it can easily be shown to be a social construct, its defences so many legitimations of power, hierarchical, patriarchal, and heterosexist. In particular, if marriage is merely a social construct, there is no reason to value it beyond the particular personal or societal ends that it may serve. Faithfulness and permanence can then only be justified by a series of proximate, penultimate goods. Perhaps faithfulness and permanence may serve the fulfilment of the spouses: people are on the whole happier if they feel that their life partner is not cheating on them and that they will be there for them when the time comes. Perhaps faithfulness and permanence are on balance good for children, who may grow up more emotionally well adjusted and resilient if they are rooted in a stable home and family life. Perhaps stable marriages are good for the well-being of society, which is composed of interwoven family networks and relies on the continued reproduction of responsible citizens.

However, none of these proximate goods can finally justify faithfulness and permanence being essential to the nature of marriage. To be sure, the well-being of married partners, of their children, and of the wider society are basic human goods. But they are contingently related to faithfulness and permanence. Spouses may fall out, and their individual or joint good may be served by separating. Children eventually grow up, and their emotional needs may not be quite so dependent on the continuing stability of their parents' relationship. And the welfare of society may not require everyone to be married or be quite as dependent on exclusive commitment to heterosexual marriage and family life as is sometimes imagined. Whether each of these is the case is of course a matter for practical investigation with a significant empirical component. But that is precisely the point: if faithfulness and permanence are only justified because they are necessary for achieving other goods, they lose their categorical force. If our marriage is not doing either of us any good and we both might do better with other partners, why should we stick with it? Why should the undeniable need for some level of social stability mean that my life should be sacrificed to it? Arguments for faithfulness and permanence will of course always have some weight, for which we may be grateful, but once they are shown to be based on proximate, contingent goods, they can never have the categorical force they are given in marriage. It is one thing to say that I pledge my troth so long as it suits our well-being, and that of our children and of wider society, another to say that I pledge my troth *because that is what marriage is.*

This theological context makes intelligible the goods of faithfulness and permanence, therefore. But it also gives final intelligibility to the good of procreation. We habitually talk of the 'gift' of a new child, and rightly so. The sense of gift at the birth of a child is not merely a sense of relief that despite the ever-present possibilities of infertility or miscarriage a child has in fact been born, though no doubt relief is among the feelings that parents may have. Nor is it simply a sense of amazement at the intricacies of embryological and foetal development that can produce such a complex new being, though no doubt many parents may also feel something of that. Rather, behind the talk of gift is a sense of awed wonder – shared even among those not inclined to think there is anyone to give the gift – which in a very loose sense we might call metaphysical: once there was nothing, but now there is a new life, a new centre of being and consciousness, a whole new world!

We might be tempted to think of this sense of wonder as explicable in evolutionary terms, that the parents' joy – or perhaps more tellingly, that of the grandparents – is just an excrescence of human evolutionary development, an overspill of the successful passing on of genes. But for Christian theology new life is not just a biological event to be understood in terms of evolution and evolutionary psychology. Rather evolution itself is to be understood as a created reflection of the divine gratuity: procreation is not just biology, but is itself also a sign of the divine goodness. The miracle of procreation is a reflection of the miracle of creation, a participation by created beings, in a way appropriate to created beings, in the original gift of creation itself.[2] Indeed this might help to make intelligible why God created human beings and not just angels. If God had wished for creatures simply to love and worship him, to fill the ranks of the choirs of heaven, then angels would have sufficed for the purpose. But one decisive difference between human beings and angels is that angels are incapable of procreation; that is, they are incapable of experiencing for themselves the joy of participating in a creaturely way in the gift of creation itself, and therefore of sharing in God's own joy in creation.

Eschatology and the intelligibility of celibacy

The goods of marriage are created goods, therefore, and they are simultaneously ways in which human beings may reflect and participate in the divine life. However, Christ is not only the one through whom the creation was made, he is also the one in whom the creation is fulfilled. And the fulfilment of creation is not only its repristination, but also its transformation. The eschatological theme in the New Testament and in Christian theology is not simply about returning to the original creation or repeating it, but also an indication that creation has a good beyond itself. Mere restoration of creation would open us up to an endless recurrence of creation, fall and re-creation, a cyclical fate of everlasting metaphysical restlessness rather than a destiny of eternal fulfilment in God. Rather, the resurrection points us towards the profound

---

2 For this theological account of evolutionary biology, see Conor Cunningham, *Darwin's Pious Idea: Why the Ultra-Darwinists and Creationists Both Get It Wrong*, Grand Rapids, MI: Eerdmans, 2010.

newness of what God has done in Christ. In the resurrection God affirms the creation even as he also transforms it into something creation could never achieve of itself. One sign of this is given in the depiction of Christ's resurrected body in the Gospels. On the one hand his body is never less than physical: he is not a ghost, but is quite pointedly shown as breaking bread, preparing breakfast, eating fish, and so on; on the other, he is capable of appearing to disciples through the locked doors of a house, and disappearing just as mysteriously. To borrow a phrase from N. T. Wright, his body is 'transphysical', both fully physical and never less than physical, but yet also somehow more than physical, occupying a space of possibilities beyond the natural.[3] Just as Christ's resurrection participates in and indeed inaugurates a new order, so also we may say that creation is pointed beyond itself to a reality that lies beyond its own immanent potential.[4]

What does the eschatological fulfilment of creation mean for our understanding of marriage? At the beginning of this chapter we considered one of Jesus' principal teachings on marriage, which refers back to creation and the Genesis narratives. One of his other principal teachings on marriage, presented in different versions in all three of the Synoptic Gospels, looks forward to the resurrection and the nature of the resurrection life. It comes in response to a question from the Sadducees, who did not believe in the resurrection and were evidently deploying a standard conundrum to bamboozle those who disputed their views. Which of seven brothers will a woman be married to in the resurrection, when she had been married to each of them in succession in obedience to the Levirate law of the remarriage of the widows of childless marriages, as found in Deuteronomy 25.5–10? Jesus responds with a teaching about marriage in the resurrection:

---

3 N. T. Wright, *The Resurrection of the Son of God*, London: SPCK, 2003, pp. 477–8.

4 For this understanding of the moral significance of the resurrection, see in general Oliver O'Donovan, *Resurrection and Moral Order: An Outline for Evangelical Ethics*, second edition, Leicester: InterVarsity Press, 1994, esp. chs 1–3.

Those who belong to this age marry and are given in marriage; but those who are considered worthy of a place in that age and in the resurrection from the dead neither marry nor are given in marriage. Indeed they cannot die any more, because they are like angels and are children of God, being children of the resurrection. (Luke 20.34–6; cf. Matt. 22.23–33; Mark 12.18–27)

The assumption behind this otherwise somewhat puzzling passage is that marriage is instituted to deal with the problem that people die. For the Jewish people of the period the question was how the family line, and thus the people of God as a whole, was to be sustained over time. For a people whose founding patriarch had been promised descendants as numerous as the sands on the seashore, and whose law was given that they might live long in the land they were to possess, to be assured of future generations was to be assured of God's continued blessing, that God's faithfulness would not cease at one's death. And in turn, to be fruitful and multiply required marriage. But what happens in the resurrection, when death shall be no more? If there is no death, the sustenance of the people of God no longer requires future generations to be born; and if there is no need for future generations to be born, there is no need for marriage. In other words, despite marriage having been so central to creation, marrying and giving in marriage will no longer figure in the life of the resurrection. Where there is resurrection, there is no death; where there is no death, there is no need for birth; where there is no birth, there is no need for marriage. 'Where there is death, there is marriage', wrote St John Chrysostom in the fourth century, crisply summing up the situation.[5]

The potential theological significance of this cannot be overstated. What was crucial to the whole creation understanding of human beings, namely the nexus of marriage and procreation, will in the eschatological fulfilment of creation become redundant. The entire edifice of human relationships built round the becoming one flesh of man and woman and the expression of this

---

5 John Chrysostom, *On Virginity*, 14.6.

in the one flesh of the child will no longer be integral to human existence. Somehow a created world of which marriage and the birth of children are crucial defining features will be fulfilled in a resurrected world in which neither is present.

To fill this out, let us look at the person of Christ. We saw earlier from Colossians 1.15ff. that Christ is the one through whom all things were made. A similar point can be drawn out in relation to the creation of human beings in the image of God. While in Genesis 1.26–27 humankind is made in the image of God, according to God's likeness, so in Colossians 1.15 the Son is revealed as 'the image of the invisible God, the firstborn of all creation'. For Paul, Adam is a 'type of the one who was to come' (Rom. 5.14), and Christ is the fulfilment. While Paul tends to draw out the parallels between Adam and Christ – in Adam all die, but in Christ all will be made alive (1 Cor. 15.22) – it is clear that the eschatological fulfilment of Adam in Christ indicates a resituating of the Genesis account of Adam. Rather than being an independent creation, Adam prefigures Christ. Christ is not just the numerical successor of Adam, but also the one to whom Adam points. He is not just another human being, but the one in whom Adam's humanity is fulfilled.

This in turn implies a resituating of what it means to be in the image of God. Throughout the history of Christian interpretation of Genesis 1 there has been much dispute about what being in the image of God consists in, each age finding in the image of God what it has most valued about itself. For Aquinas it consisted in human rationality, as that which distinguishes humankind from other animals. For many in modern times it has been taken to refer to human capacities for relationship. For Karl Barth, noting the immediate context of Genesis 1.27, it was specifically the fact of being created male and female. However we decide that question, we should note that it is probable that Genesis shared the common view of the ancient Near East that kings were made in the divine image, and as divine image-bearers ruled on God's behalf. Thus for Adam to be in the image of God was for him to have authority over the rest of creation and to exercise stewardship of it on behalf of God. Correspondingly, Christ, who rises where

Adam fails to exercise authority and so falls, is the one who has 'all things in subjection under his feet', as Paul confirms in 1 Corinthians 15.27, echoing Psalm 8.6's version of the Genesis picture. All the different answers to the question of what the image of God consists in are best understood as answering the substantive question: in virtue of what is humankind given the role of rulership? Why is it that the role of rulership is given to human beings and not to any other creatures?

The Genesis passage gives us no solid clues in answer to these questions. Most accounts of the image ostensibly derived from it owe their results more to theological construction than strict exegesis. However, the passage does speak to the question of one of the necessary prerequisites of rulership which makes rulership possible, namely procreation. One precondition for ruling the earth is filling it, and filling it requires being fruitful and multiplying. The command to have dominion over the other creatures in verse 28 therefore is immediately preceded by God's blessing, together with the command to be fruitful and multiply, to fill the earth and subdue it in verse 27. And this surely makes sense of the specific reference to male and female in the words that immediately precede in turn, 'male and female he created them' (v. 26). Human beings are made male and female, not because Genesis is answering a question about gender in the being of God (though equally this passage does not foreclose such possibilities), nor solely because being human is about fundamental relationality (true though that may be), nor even because of something vaguely complementary about maleness and femaleness. Rather it is the very concrete orientation of sexual differentiation to procreation that brings out the logic of the passage: being created in a relationship of male and female is what enables humankind to procreate; being able to procreate enables it to fill the earth and subdue it; being able to rule the earth enables it to fulfil its role as bearing the image of God.

We can now see how Christ resituates Adam's imaging of God. The first *adam* may be created male and female, and thereby ordained and rendered able to procreate. But the last Adam, the one who unlike the first Adam does succeed in having all things placed under his feet, does not do so by procreation. Jesus Christ, in whom creation is being renewed (cf. Col. 3.10–11), points the way to a different order in which marriage is to be fulfilled. Jesus' mother and brothers are not those to whom he is biologically related, but whoever hears the word of God and does it (Luke 8.21; Mark 3.34). Unlike the old covenant, in which membership of the chosen community was determined by shared ancestral blood, membership in the new covenant community is determined by sharing in the blood of Christ. Life in the community of the resurrection is life in which the hope of children is no longer intrinsic to the community's identity. Human flourishing has been given a profound reorientation: full humanity, full participation in the imaging of God, is possible without marriage, without procreation, indeed without being sexually active. Celibacy, in other words, has become an appropriate stance for those who wish to live in the new age.

And so, fittingly, the historical Jesus appears never to have been married, nor to have had biological children. Paul likewise seems to have been unmarried, certainly by the time he wrote 1 Corinthians 7: his wish 'that all were as I am' (v. 7) indicates his preference that followers of Christ would likewise not be married. In view of the shortage of the time, even those who have wives should be as though they had none (v. 29): he would rather that those whom God has called were anxious about the affairs of the Lord, rather than anxious about the affairs of the world, how to please their wife or husband (vv. 32–35). The form of the present world is passing away, and the point of remaining unmarried is to enable followers of Christ to devote themselves to the works of the Lord with their loyalties undivided.

Paul's stance may look pragmatic, as if he adopts a position that is most suited to the organizational needs of the Church's mission. And the thought may not be unlike that of those eunuchs of whom Jesus speaks, 'who have made themselves eunuchs for the sake of the kingdom of heaven' (Matt. 19.11). But we should be clear that it is part of a pattern of thought throughout the New Testament which does not see marriage and family life as part of the eschatological future. Whereas conventional Jewish eschatology depicted the age to come as 'a time of abundance and fruitful families',[6] this is precisely the option that Jesus and Paul refuse.

Indeed it is striking that there is almost nothing in the New Testament which actively encourages having children, nor is pro-creation ever given as a reason for Christians to seek marriage. Children are of course welcomed by Jesus, and no one may enter the Kingdom except as a child; and the existence of children is taken for granted in the household instructions found in some of the Epistles (e.g. Eph. 6.1–4; Col. 3.20–21). But the case for actively *having* children, as opposed to welcoming or giving instruction to those children that already exist, is very hard to make from the pages of the New Testament. The only possible counter-example is the ambiguous and ostensibly un-Lutheran suggestion that women 'will be saved through childbearing' (1 Tim. 2.15), which may be an internal New Testament response to a misunderstanding of 1 Corinthians 7 that having children was actively sinful, or may simply mean that women will give birth safely. It is not surprising therefore that the early post-apostolic Church thought that renun-ciation of marriage and the family was an eminently appropriate way of pointing to the radical nature of the new order instituted in the resurrection. Over against a predominant set of expectations, both in Judaism and in contemporary Greco-Roman society and in innumerable societies before and since, that a person's identity was secured through preservation into posterity of their family line or nation or race, the early Christians abandoned their invest-ment in earthly ambition in favour of a new society, a departure which was made intelligible for them because of the extravagant reality of the resurrection.

A twofold witness

In view of all this it would be reasonable to deduce that the demands of the Kingdom simply override all other norms, that

---

6 William Loader, *The New Testament on Sexuality,* Grand Rapids, MI: Eerdmans, 2012, p. 494.

the eschatological order erases the created order. The new age has come, it might be thought, and the newness of the new creation represents the abandonment of the former creation. And all of this would be of a piece with the radical demands made of those who seek to follow Christ: for the sake of the Kingdom they must leave home, their wives and families (Luke 18.28–30).

But the New Testament does not abandon marriage. Jesus' message may represent a radical resituating of marriage and procreation, and life in the age to come may better be witnessed to by celibacy than by marriage, but he does also reaffirm the created demand for marital permanence over against easy permission of divorce. In 1 Corinthians 7 Paul, despite his clear preference that Christians be single, also pronounces that marriage is not sinful ('if you marry, you do not sin' (7.28)). Each man should have his own wife and each woman her own husband, even if only to avoid sexual immorality (7.2): it is better to marry than to burn with passion (7.9). None of these grudging concessions quite represents the ringing endorsement of marriage that liturgists might have hoped for when looking for a suitable New Testament verse to open the marriage service – though at least Jesus was present at the wedding of Cana in Galilee (and thereby 'adorned and beautified' marriage with his presence and first miracle, as the *Book of Common Prayer* had it), and marriage can still be modelled on the relationship of Christ and the Church, as we have seen.

Christian eschatology therefore does not represent a denial of the goods of creation. We may and should rejoice when couples choose to marry, and we may and should welcome children into the world. Even if the days of marriage are numbered, it is not wrong for Christians to marry. But marriage no longer carries the aura of inevitability: the New Testament message of eschatological disruption undermines assumptions of this-worldly stability and permanence. Likewise the significance of procreation has changed. Instead of reinforcing expectations about the continuity of generations into the indefinite future, children have become a sign that God has not yet given up on the world: in the midst of the ever-present possibility of judgement, children are a sign of God's continuing goodness. Indeed, now that after the incarnation children are no longer essential for our identity, we may affirm that the birth of every single child has become yet more evidently what they always were, namely a sign of the divine gratuity.

The sense of an eschatological context but also of the continuing goodness of creation has bequeathed to the Christian Church from the start an irrevocable tension between the claims of celibacy and of marriage. But we also find the resolution of this tension at the very start, in the notion of vocation or calling. In 1 Corinthians 7, Paul commands that each is to stay in the condition in which they were called, slave or free, married or unmarried: 'let each of you lead the life that the Lord has assigned, to which God called you' (7.17).[7] It would be easy to suppose that the idea of vocation was the unusual occurrence, as if marriage were the norm and celibacy the calling, as if to some it is given to become eunuchs for the sake of the Kingdom, but everyone else is to carry on as before. But for Paul the logic of calling is one that applies to all Christians. All are called, and all have their gifting: 'each has a particular gift from God, one having one kind and another a different kind' (7.7). Celibacy is certainly a calling for which a particular gift is given, and for which a particular gift is needed. But so is marriage: what was once taken for granted as 'natural' has for the follower of Christ become contingent, a vocation for which also a particular gift is given and for which a particular gift is needed.

The balance between celibacy and marriage has been struck in different ways in different eras. The early and medieval Church prized celibacy above marriage, and even if this was without

---

7 The primary reference of 'calling' for Paul may be the call into faith rather than the call to a particular 'vocation' or condition such as marriage or singleness, slavery or freedom; that is, each is to lead the life they had been assigned when they heard the call of the gospel. However, the fact that the Lord has 'assigned' a life to each (7.17), and that each has a particular gift (7.7), does suggest that Paul is operating also with a particularized sense of the divine intention for an individual's life; and it is this which I take to license the use of the word 'calling' both here and throughout this book. See further Anthony C. Thiselton, *The First Epistle to the Corinthians: A Commentary on the Greek Text*, Grand Rapids, MI: Eerdmans, 2000, pp. 548–50.

question unhealthily seasoned by a persistent distrust of the irrational nature of sexuality and of women who embodied it, it is hard not to see this preference for celibacy as having elements of an authentically New Testament character. The Reformers by contrast were suspicious of the works-righteousness implicit in claims to the superior virtue and heavenly reward of the celibate and eloquent in their denunciation of the sexual scandals caused by those who evidently did not have the gift of celibacy after all: 'not one in a thousand' had been granted such a miraculous state, opined Luther.[8] Yet if we in the contemporary Church have a need now, one might say that it is to recover the significance of authentic celibacy. Against the heritage of Protestant ideals of the family, against post- and sub-Freudian assumptions about the necessity of a healthy sex life for psychological wholeness, against the late modern capitalist consumerization of sexuality, a renewed understanding of the theological significance of celibacy and vowed singleness is surely essential to the Church's truthful witness.

But does it follow that the Church may recognize only two callings? Or might it be that there could be a third? It is to this possibility that we now turn.

---

8 Martin Luther, 'The Estate of Marriage', in *Luther's Works*, vol. 45, ed. Walther I. Brandt, Philadelphia, PA: Fortress Press, 1962, pp. 11–49 at p. 21.

2

Covenant Partnership

The coming of Christ resituates marriage. Not only does it make evident that marriage may not be grounded untheologically outside an understanding of God's covenant relationship with us, it also bursts the seams of marriage and points to a new eschatological order in which marrying and giving in marriage, and therefore procreation, are no longer part. Marriage remains a good of creation, as does its procreative orientation. But now, since the advent of Christ, celibacy has become a standing sign that a new order has been inaugurated, one in which marriage has a continuing role, albeit one that is time-limited.

What are we to make of the claim that marriage and procreation are no longer taken for granted as necessary for those who are in Christ and are called to live appropriately to the new aeon? Throughout Christian history there has been an assumption that there are at most two callings, to marriage or to celibacy, in accordance with the New Testament pattern which never envisages any possibility of a third. However, we need to ask whether celibacy might not be the only other option opened up by the coming of Christ. Might it be that certain other kinds of relationship are also made possible which were theologically speaking never possible before? In this chapter I explore the idea of a third vocation, which would be marked by faithfulness, a commitment to permanence and by kinds of fruitfulness other than biological procreation. Such relationships need not be homosexual; in fact the first pointers to the possibility of such a partnership that I will discuss are heterosexual. But in principle they could be same-sex, and for that reason I want to start off by outlining some problems with one common kind of defence of same-sex relationships which suggest that we need to address the issue of same-sex partnerships in a different way.

Are same-sex relationships given in creation?

A kind of argument frequently found in theological proposals for same-sex relationships goes something like this. Although same-sex relationships are not heterosexual and are not intrinsically open to procreation, they can embody the same virtues as marriage. In particular they can display the same loving commitments to faithfulness and permanence – and may produce many of the same fruits – as marriage. Of course, not all same-sex relationships do, any more than do all heterosexual married relationships, but many do display such virtues and in so doing they are capable of reflecting God's covenant faithfulness towards us in the same way as does marriage. The sex of the partners does not intrinsically matter, either because the fundamental moral issue is the quality of relationship between the partners rather than their sex, or because sex and/or gender are intrinsically unstable or deconstructible or are in some other way insufficiently determinable, perhaps because of the existence of intersex or similar conditions, or because we should not draw moral conclusions from the physiological and/or social categories that sex or gender are taken to refer to. And this assertion of the unimportance of the sex of the partners is then read back into creation, so that no significance can be attributed to the creation of human beings as male and female, beyond the fact of their being characterized by generic but ungendered relationality.

I am not unsympathetic to a number of aspects of this kind of position, and will be arguing some similar points myself. But as typically presented it runs several significant risks from a theological point of view. One is that it is in danger of denying the goodness of the material creation. A consistent theme throughout the Jewish and Christian Scriptures is that the material world is a source of delight alike for Creator ('God saw everything that he had made, and indeed, it was very good' (Gen. 1.31)) and for creature ('I praise you, for I am fearfully and wonderfully made'

(Ps. 139.14)). This includes not merely the materiality of creation but also the form in which it is made; indeed properly speaking there is no such thing as unformed matter, that is, matter that is not the material substrate of something. The effort to escape the formed matter of creation, including the form of the body, is one of the characteristics of the various gnostic and spiritualizing movements that pervaded the climate within which the early Church grew up. In a different but analogous way, escape from matter is one aspect of the modern world's efforts to be rid of the burdens of mortality by means of technology: it is a significant task of contemporary Christian discernment to distinguish the proper goals of medicine in alleviating suffering and contributing to the health of the body from the desire to abandon finitude altogether. To be sure in relation to sex and gender we should be very wary of naive claims to read off the nature of sexual difference from our biological constitution, let alone of making correlations between biological sex and socially ascribed gender, as some decades of critical gender studies have demonstrated. And we should certainly question the theological use of the creation narratives to pathologize bodies that do not conform to exclusively male/female norms. But to abandon the notion of sexual differentiation entirely in favour of a generic relationality indifferent to one's sex, or to deny that there is a spectrum of biological sex on which human beings are situated, is to run the risk of denying any meaning at all to the phrase 'male and female he created them', as well as of ignoring evolutionary biological claims about sexual reproduction that illustrate it. However we decide to circumscribe or interpret our understandings of maleness and femaleness, we may not evacuate the concepts of significance altogether.

Connected with this, a second concern is that this approach is in jeopardy of losing its properly theological shape. In losing its connection with the specificity of creation, it is liable to make timeless claims about human beings which fail to be anchored properly in the theological narrative of creation, incarnation and redemption. Not only do such claims lose their mooring in creation, they also sever their connection to eschatology. Theological references to covenant or to the symbolism of Christ and Church may then too easily become a theological gloss on a conceptual scheme organized along rather different lines. In particular, they may come to serve as a legitimation for modern notions of abstract individuals contracting together for reasons of mutual benefit. The end result of this trajectory is for theology to import Enlightenment contractarian understandings of marriage, in which marriage becomes a voluntary bargain struck between individuals who agree the terms on which they will enter upon, conduct and depart from their contracted relationship.[1] While not all those who pursue the line of thought I am criticizing go this far, I should make very clear, some certainly do; and we may wonder what are likely to be the downstream consequences of some intellectual decisions made much earlier on.

Third, following on from both of these, there is a concern that if this approach to same-sex relationships is extended to a defence of same-sex marriage, it will obscure the connection in creation between marriage and procreation. As we saw in Chapter 1, procreation as the fruit of the one-flesh relationship is an inseparable good of marriage in creation. But procreation as the result of their sexual union is not possible for same-sex couples, and so also marriage understood as a creation good is not possible for same-sex couples. It will not really suffice to argue in response to this that the two kinds of relationship should be treated as analogous, for example by appealing to the reasoning that, as we are happy to talk of polygamous marriages as marriages by analogy, so also we should be free to refer to same-sex marriages as marriages by analogy. For an analogy is not as such an argument, unless one can show that the analogy obtains in the relevant ways. Polygamous marriages are indeed called marriage by analogy with monogamous marriage, but we may not infer that there are no morally relevant differences between them. Similarly, of course we can easily see what people mean when they talk of 'same-sex marriage', but what they mean refers primarily to the other two

---

1 For discussion of the Enlightenment contractarian model of marriage, see John Witte Jr, *From Sacrament to Contract: Marriage, Religion, and Law in the Western Tradition*, Grand Rapids, MI: Eerdmans, 1997, esp. ch. 5.

goods of marriage and not to procreation; and procreation, I have argued, is a morally relevant difference. If we are to find a theological account of faithful and permanent same-sex relationships, it will need to be by a different route and cannot proceed by hurriedly eliding the question of procreation.

The upshot of these points is that, ironically, this approach might end up reinforcing a subterranean sense that same-sex relationships are really second-class after all. The effort to write same-sex relationships into creation narratives which are arguably only partly hospitable to them requires suppressing features that remain stubbornly visible. Rather than illuminating some core features of the moral landscape, it is in danger of casting a veil over them.

The calling to covenant partnership

In view of all this, might it not be better to recognize that while committed same-sex relationships will share certain features with marriage, they are theologically speaking *not* in fact the same and have a different place within the divine economy? Might it be that same-sex relationships have their own integrity and that this is a different integrity from that of heterosexual married relationships? By not anxiously seeking a toehold in the created order, might they be freed up to be something that marriage as a creation ordinance can never be and should not seek to be?

To explore this, let us recall that, of the three goods of marriage, procreation has become redundant, theologically speaking, for those who are in Christ. Children are still a good, we should be clear, and they remain a good to which the Church will witness until the end of time, however unpopular such a stance may well turn out to be in the future – if ecological pressures become overwhelming, for example. Likewise faithfulness and permanence also continue to be goods. But it is important to note that they are goods in a different way from procreation. For procreation is a good of creation that gains its final intelligibility from its being a participation by created beings, in a manner appropriate to created beings, in the original gift of creation itself. And just as creation has now been fulfilled in Christ, so the purpose of procreation has now been fulfilled. By contrast, faithfulness and permanence are goods that gain their final intelligibility from their witnessing to the future relationship between humankind and God that has been made real in Christ and will be revealed in its fullness in the eschaton. In other words, while the three goods are inseparable as goods of creation, the coming of Christ reveals their different logics and divergent trajectories.

This opens up the question whether, in addition to celibacy, there might be forms of non-procreative committed relationship that may also function as a kind of eschatological witness. Given that such relationships would gain their ultimate intelligibility from being a witness to God's covenant love to human beings, I propose to use the term 'covenant partnerships' for them.

How would covenant partnerships be characterized? Like marriages, they also would be marked by three goods. First, those entering upon them would be committed to faithfulness. Just as Christ gave himself up for the Church, so also the partners would commit themselves not only negatively to excluding sexual relationships with all others, but would each be actively committed to giving themselves up for and nurturing the other in love. Second, they would embody a commitment to permanence. Just as God, despite his anger at Israel's unfaithfulness, repeatedly commits himself to them, so covenant partnerships would be constituted and sustained by mutual commitments of the partners to each other until death did them part. Third, instead of biological pro-creativity, they would be characterized by other forms of fruitfulness. Since such relationships are eschatologically grounded, they would take their orientation from the demands of the Kingdom. In line with Paul's aspirations in 1 Corinthians 7, they would be freed to be anxious about the affairs of the Lord, how to please the Lord; they could not be self-enclosed or self-satisfied, but would be open to the call of charity beyond themselves. Echoing in the new eschatological context God's original declaration about Adam that it is not good for human beings to be alone, their relationship would enable each to be a helper to the other, making possible a degree of fruitfulness in the service of the Kingdom that might not have been possible for them as individuals separately.

The precise forms of fruitfulness each couple was called to would depend on their times and circumstances. Although they would not have children as a result of their sexual relationship, this would not preclude their bringing up children: the role of adopting or fostering, for example, would be a prime example of fruitfulness. Alternatively, if they did not have responsibility for children, they might be in a position that those who are committed to the care of children would be unable to emulate; for example, being mission partners in contexts that those with children might find difficult, opening up their homes to provide hospitality for those in need, devoting time and energy to environmental causes. The length of the list is restricted only by the limits of the imagination and in practice would be expanded indefinitely by those who had committed to covenant partnership and were exploring its possibilities for themselves.

Such covenant partnerships would be a vocation, we should be clear. Not everyone is capable of such a relationship, but only those to whom it is given. Not everyone is able to live in a relationship where it was known from the outset that children would not be the fruit of the partners' one-flesh union. Not everyone would find it so easy to sustain a relationship committed to permanence in cases where there were no children to strengthen the partnership. But each has a particular gift from God, one having one kind and another a different kind (1 Cor. 7.7; cf. Eph. 4.7; 1 Pet. 4.10); where there is a call, so also will there be the gift to fulfil it. And the gift each is given will mark out the path of discipleship and of growth in holiness to which each is called. Just as for marriage, each of the callings brings with it its own demand and its own particular path of sanctification.

Childless marriages

What pointers might there be to the category of covenant partnership? I want to start off from an example whose significance will not be obvious to those reared on contemporary Protestant or Anglican expectations of marriage: namely deliberately childless marriages, where the couple enter upon marriage with the express understanding between themselves that they will not have children as a result of their sexual relationship. I draw attention to these not in order to make an abstract criticism of them; on the contrary it is precisely because they *can* embody something theologically meaningful that I wish to defend them.

Now there may be reasons for choosing deliberate childlessness that we might wish to question. Perhaps the couple favour it because they would prefer to enjoy the stability, the sense of belonging, the social status and the comfort of marriage, but without the constraints – the drain on energy and time and the expense – of having children. We might wonder whether such a relationship is in danger of becoming consumerist, self-absorbed and inhospitable, an *égoisme à deux* which on the face of it stands against some of the central commitments of Christian discipleship.

But equally there are some prima facie extremely good reasons for a married couple to choose to forgo having children. After very careful moral consideration, they may feel that there would be what the moral theological tradition has called 'grave reasons' for not doing so. For example, there may run in the family of one or both of them a serious genetic disorder which they would prefer not to pass on to a child. Or they may believe that they are called to some form of Christian ministry in which the nurturing and education of children was not likely to be propitious – certain kinds of missionary work, for example. Perhaps one of them has a chronic mental health condition, or they have other good reasons to think that their competence to bring up children adequately is liable to be significantly compromised. Perhaps the woman has embarked on marriage in her forties or fifties, and is unsure about the increased risk of serious medical complications in having children later in life. Or, a consideration that is going to be of increasing salience, the couple may feel a concern about the additional burden on the planet's scarce resources that having children will bring: children born in richer countries consume the world's goods and contribute to climate change and destruction of the world's resources in prodigious disproportion to their numbers, and couples concerned for the welfare of future generations may well feel that the path of discipleship requires them to forsake having children.

It is not my purpose here to consider the detailed morality of any such decisions, either in general or in particular cases. The point rather is to illustrate that some couples may choose not to have children for reasons that are not in any obvious way selfish or consumerist or narcissistic, but may have been subjected to considerable moral interrogation and self-examination. These decisions may have been made faithfully, prayerfully, and with the full support of the church community. The partnership such couples embark on may be marked by complete fidelity and commitment to permanence. Indeed they are conventionally called marriage and have the legal and social status of marriage. And yet in their deliberate childlessness they reject one of the three goods of marriage.

To see what is at stake in such a rejection, we should recall the connection of marriage as a creation good, on the one hand, and procreation, on the other. As we saw in Chapter 1, the assumption behind Jesus' teaching that in the resurrection people will be like the angels in heaven is that marriage is intrinsically related to procreation: in the resurrection life there will be no death, and therefore no need for birth, and therefore no need for marriage. If marriage was morally possible without an openness to procreation, Jesus' argument would not have gone through: he could simply have declared that in the resurrection marriages will be childless. Moreover the connection between marriage and procreation is not contingent, based on a general empirical observation that the one always (or rather, usually) leads to the other. Rather the opening chapters of Genesis show that the connection between the two is an inextricable part of the point of marriage: being created male and female, and the joining in the one-flesh union of marriage that this is related to, is intrinsically connected to being blessed, being fruitful and multiplying. Procreation is not the only good of marriage as a created ordinance, let us be clear, but it is an intrinsic and inseparable good of it.

For this reason, the mainstream of Christian tradition has always held that every marriage should be open to new life. Deliberate infertility for the duration of a marriage strikes at the heart of the historic Christian understanding of marriage. On the understanding that marriage is defined as the kind of relationship constituted by the three goods of faithfulness, permanence and procreation, it is no more justifiable to enter upon marriage deliberately intending not to have children than to enter marriage deliberately intending not to be faithful or not to be married until death does part. Among the Western Churches the Roman Catholic Church has held on to this with most clarity; indeed it has further interpreted this to mean that not only should every marriage be open to new life, but 'every marital act' as well – a rejection not just of deliberately childless marriages but of contraception altogether, an issue I will return to in the next chapter. By contrast the Anglican Communion departed from this at the Lambeth Conference of 1930: Resolution 15 allowed that there might be a 'clearly felt moral obligation to limit *or avoid* parenthood' but simultaneously a 'morally sound reason for avoiding complete abstinence', and declared that the method of contraception should be decided on Christian principles.[2] And sentiments about the choice not to have children at all are to be found in Church of England House of Bishops statements right up to the present day.

As it happens, official Roman Catholic teaching does permit deliberately childless marriages, at least in a limited number of cases, provided that this is undertaken for moral reason, with serious motives and in conformity with the Church's teaching on contraception. Pope Pius XII gave as examples of appropriate circumstances of deliberately childless marriages a couple who were carriers of known genetic defects which they might pass on to children or a woman whose life might be threatened by pregnancy. But it is evident that these cases were expected to be extremely rare; there is no concession to the thought that whether to have children or not is simply a matter of choice.

It may be that the Lambeth 1930 resolution could also be read in a similar way, given the emphasis on a 'clearly felt moral obligation'

---

2 http://www.lambethconference.org/resolutions/1930/1930-15.cfm (accessed 24 April 2014); italics added.

as the grounds for avoiding having children. This would certainly be closer to the historic Christian understanding of marriage than much current Anglican (and more broadly Protestant) practice, and there is a very strong case for returning to it. How churches might call into question the culture of choice with regard to deliberate childlessness, and recall their congregations to a theologically defensible position in the light of the tradition, is a matter for careful pastoral wisdom. But without some such recovery the inequity between the churches' treatment of married couples and their treatment of lesbian and gay relationships will continue to justify the perceptions of hypocrisy: one kind of falling short of the ideals of biblical and traditional teaching on marriage and sexuality is ignored, while another is greeted with synodical motions calling for a call to repentance and the exercise of compassion.

However, even if the churches were to restore a pastoral practice in relation to deliberately childless marriages which is more in keeping with the tradition, an underlying question remains untouched. For these relationships still remain conceived on a deficit model, defined by what they lack. Might we not be able to imagine an alternative response to the place of deliberately childless marriages that hints at something altogether more constructive and hopeful? Might it not be the case, we could enquire, that there is concealed in some such examples the germ of a different kind of calling, not strictly to marriage in creation as traditionally understood, but to something subtly and importantly different? That a relationship deliberately did not have children, far from being an implicit transgression of creation norms, might be precisely the qualification needed to allow other sorts of ministries to prosper and other outworkings of charity to bear fruit. If we were to choose this latter route, affirming that such relationships should be recognized under the category of vocation, rather than tacitly diminishing or patronizing or excluding them, we would be offering a constructive theological account of what otherwise reinforces an economy of marginalization.

In addition to those who embark on deliberately childless marriages, might it be that this understanding of vocation could help us to shed light on the situation of two kinds of marriages that are also childless, but contingently rather than deliberately so? The first of these two kinds is that of couples who enter on marriage knowing that they will certainly not have children, on the grounds of the age or known infertility of one or both of the couple. Again, in referring to couples of this kind, my purpose is not to put their relationship in question; on the contrary it is exactly because such relationships are prima facie morally unproblematic that the issues they pose for the historic understanding of marriage deserve attention. Understanding that procreativity is part of the calling of marriage, they may still be fully open to having children in a hypothetical if somewhat quixotic sense, even though rationally they know that this will not happen – short of a special visitation from the Lord of the kind granted to Abraham and Sarah or Zechariah and Elizabeth. They would not be deliberately thwarting creation: it is just that a post-menopausal body or the result of treatment for testicular cancer or similar contingent circumstances have made it factually impossible. Conventionally and socially these have widely been accepted as marriage, and inasmuch as in some very etiolated and counterfactual sense they are open to procreation as one of the three goods of marriage, one can see why the case has been made for this to be correct theologically.

Yet even if those Roman Catholic priests were technically ill-informed who were from time to time rumoured to have refused to marry couples in such circumstances, something in their instincts may not have been entirely erroneous.[3] In the first place, if marriage is in part constituted by its procreativity and yet procreation is not possible, it is not clear what feature of marriage will ensure that such couples will be oriented to the good beyond themselves that is ordinarily embodied in children. Children symbolize, and in their demands on their parents they actualize, an openness to

---

3 Official Roman Catholic teaching distinguishes infertility, the inability to conceive children for the kinds of reasons given, from impotence, the permanent inability to have sexual intercourse, whether on the part of the man or the woman. The former is not an impediment to a valid marriage; the latter (the text-book case being quadriplegia) is an impediment, though in practice the benefit of any doubt may be given to the couple. Impotence would of course not be an impediment to covenant partnership.

hospitality that prevents marriages collapsing into an egoistic and complacent coupledom. Second, if the sexual relationship of such couples has any meaning at all, it must be something different from the meaning that is conferred by the knowledge that it is related to the factual possibility of having children. However we are to understand sexual union in their case, it has to be conceptualized in terms that acknowledge its lack of procreative capacity as a matter of fact.

The second kind of contingently childless marriage is that of those who discover their infertility only after they have embarked on marriage. These couples may be wholeheartedly open to having children; indeed nothing may be more devoutly desired, and they may eventually decide to turn to IVF or other reproductive technologies to assist them, with a considerable drain on their time, money and emotions. Again (I leave aside here issues about the ethics of IVF and other kinds of assisted reproduction) there is no question that these should be regarded as marriage, and that childlessness is not theologically a sufficient reason for ending a marriage. As Augustine maintained, lack of procreation in a marriage is not a cause for dissolving the bond of permanence: the quest to have children does not override one's duty to one's spouse, nor does it render him or her an instrument to one's desire for progeny, disposable in case of failure to perform – notwithstanding the views of the first Supreme Head of the Church of England on the matter. Yet of course it is only too understandable for couples who find themselves to be infertile to see themselves as in some sense incomplete and unfulfilled. 'Give me children, or I shall die,' weeps Rachel (Gen. 30.1): it is unsurprising that infertility is associated with increased levels of marriage breakdown.

Psychologically one of the ways of coming to terms with the grief of not being able to have children of one's own is learning to accept that there can be other forms of fulfilment of a couple's relationship than birth children. Not least among these is the possibility of adopting or fostering children or of playing a greater role in the upbringing of other children in wider family and friendship circles; though couples may also realize other ways of channelling the love and the instincts for parenting than immediately through care for children. Reflecting on their lives, such couples may well say that not having birth children led them along a different and perhaps more challenging path than the one they were expecting; they may additionally conclude (as many do) that adopting or fostering was the best thing they ever did, and that the silver lining turned out to be rather larger than the cloud. Theologically we might interpret this as the dawning recognition of a different vocation from the one they originally expected, one that takes place within a married relationship but that is lit up from an understanding of covenant partnerships that does not presume procreativity to be normative.

Same-sex relationships

Each of these three cases illuminates different aspects of marriage and different ways in which the theology of covenant partnership might helpfully be brought to bear. Deliberately childless marriages raise the question whether there might be a genuinely different vocation, namely to non-procreative partnership. Marriages that are contingently infertile due to, say, age suggest that in certain circumstances sexual intimacy must mean something that is separable from its actual procreative capacity. And marriages that are discovered to be involuntarily infertile could help couples to learn that their marriage could become something subtly but importantly different from what they had initially imagined.

There are no prizes for guessing where the argument is going. Might it be that same-sex couples could also form covenant partnerships? Could they also bear eschatological witness to the goods of faithfulness, permanence and fruitfulness, and thus participate in the corporate ecclesial discernment of vocation, in which some are called to bear witness to the goods of creation, others to creation's fulfilment in the coming Kingdom? I have just discussed the possibility that a deliberately childless marriage might point us to the idea of a covenant partnership and that this understanding of vocation might usefully illuminate two different kinds of contingently childless marriages. But these are all examples of heterosexual relationship, which suggests an important conclusion, namely that if we are to introduce the category of covenant partnership at all, the fundamental distinction it connotes is not between heterosexual and homosexual relationships but between procreative and non-procreative relationships. For a variety of reasons we may have become used to understanding the basic contrast in a way that problematizes same-sex partnerships, but in the light of this more significant distinction between procreative and non-procreative, itself theologically grounded in the contrast between those relationships which witness to the goods of creation and those which witness to the eschatological future, a rather different vista opens up.

However, even if we accept the possibility of non-procreative covenant relationships, there are still some crucial questions to be answered before they could be used to justify same-sex sexual partnerships, or partnerships involving transsexuals or people with intersex conditions. Among them: if we are to regard marriage in creation as necessarily heterosexual, what are the reasons for this, and do they apply to all committed sexual relationships – or might covenant partnerships somehow escape this constraint? Is sex not somehow intrinsically related to procreation, and does this not mean that all sexual relationships must be heterosexual – or can sex have meaning even when separated from an openness to procreation? Even if we endorsed homosexual covenant partnerships, could we not do so without endorsing their sexual expression – or is sexual intimacy legitimate within same-sex covenant partnerships? In Chapter 3 I begin to explore these questions.

3

Sexual Differentiation, Sex and Procreation

The vocation to covenant partnership shares with marriage the goods of faithfulness and permanence, but differs in that it is oriented to forms of fruitfulness other than procreation. That covenant partnerships are not inherently procreative does not mean that they would never involve the raising of children, only that children would not be a result of the couple's sexual relationship. As we saw in the last chapter, such relationships might in principle be homosexual as much as heterosexual: the fundamental distinction within committed relationships is not whether they are heterosexual or homosexual, but whether they are procreative or non-procreative in orientation.

However, it would be quite possible to accept that there is a theological case for the category of covenant partnerships, but to deny that these could be sexually active homosexual relationships. Marriage in creation after all is sexually differentiated, it might be argued, and this should apply to all committed, sexually expressed relationships; moreover, monastic traditions show that there can be vowed commitments to various kinds of same-sex relationships which are not sexually active. In this chapter I will address the two crucial dimensions of the objection that covenant partnerships may not be simultaneously same-sex and sexually active. This requires, first, investigating what the reasons are for maintaining that marriage as a creation ordinance must be heterosexual: in particular, is there a compelling case for a sexual complementarity that is not specifically connected to procreation? Second, it requires asking whether sex must always be open to procreation, or whether it might independently be related to other goods; this resolves itself in part into a consideration of the ethics of contraception.

Marriage and sexual differentiation

'Dearly beloved, we are gathered together here in the sight of God, and in the face of this Congregation, to join together this man and this woman in holy Matrimony', opens the marriage service in the *Book of Common Prayer*. As a matter of brute historical fact, the Christian tradition has known of no other kind of marriage than that between a man and a woman, and for some that is sufficient to close the case: marriage, they conclude, must be between spouses of opposing sexes, and there is no further discussion to be had. But a Christian theology that is properly alert to its responsibilities cannot rest on the mere facticity that historically marriage within the tradition has always been between a male and a female. If we are to understand the issues well, we have to think through to its roots the rationale for sexual differentiation in marriage, and to draw out the implications of this for covenant partnerships. If it turns out that the justification for sexual differentiation in marriage turns on reasons which would apply to all committed relationships, both marriage and covenant partnerships, then the possibility of specifically same-sex covenant partnerships would be ruled out: even if one accepted the arguments for non-procreative covenant partnerships that I presented in Chapter 2, they would nevertheless still have to be heterosexual. Equally if it turns out, as I will argue is the case, that the reasons for thinking that marriage should be sexually differentiated are reasons that apply only to marriage, then covenant partnerships would be freed to be either heterosexual or homosexual.

The Christian tradition offers broadly three basic kinds of reason for thinking that marriage should be sexually differentiated.[1]

---

1 Several other theological defences of sexual differentiation in marriage are to be found, but none carry the same weight as the three considered here. See in general Christopher Chenault Roberts, *Creation and Covenant: The Significance of Sexual Difference in the Moral Theology of Marriage*

The first reason is that marriage embodies a hierarchical relation-ship between the sexes. If one believes that male and female are related as superordinate to subordinate, and if one also assumes that a relationship between two superordinates or between two subordinates will lack the rightly ordered structure that a mar-riage properly needs, then one has the groundwork for an argu-ment that marriages should be heterosexual.

Evidence that the Bible endorses or assumes a hierarchical relation between the sexes can be gathered from numerous texts. In Genesis 2, for example, as we saw earlier, Eve is taken from Adam's side in order to provide a helper for him. Of course there may be reasons for mitigating the apparent force of the pas-sage: for example, one might argue that its point is to show that Adam's helper is not an animal over which he has dominion, but another of his own species with whom he is to share dominion, or that elsewhere in the Old Testament the Lord is described as being a helper to Israel, and so on. But these observations only marginally diminish the overwhelming sense that we are offered here an androcentric perspective. And in general throughout both Testaments texts come readily to hand that appear to take for granted and actively to teach that men and women are to be placed in an unequal, hierarchical relationship both in mar-riage and in social relationships more generally. For example, Ephesians 5.21–33, which we considered in Chapter 1 for its analogization of the marriage relationship to the relationship of Christ and the Church, argues that wives should be subject to their husbands since the husband is the head of the wife 'just as Christ is the head of the Church' (Eph. 5.23). Perhaps most clearly of all, 1 Corinthians 11.3–16 elaborates an argument for women wearing veils in church on the grounds that they are at the bottom end of a theological chain of being in which 'Christ is the head of every man, and the husband is the head of his wife, and God is the head of Christ' (1 Cor. 11.3). And if we turn to

---

New York: T & T Clark, 2007, for an excellent overview of the history of Christian thought on the subject. While I part from his conclusions, this should not detract from my indebtedness to his readings of the tradition.

the history of Christian theology, the same hierarchical assumptions pervade the mainstream theological tradition remorselessly, as has been chronicled time and again in several decades of feminist scholarship.

Against the apparent force of these passages, on the other hand, it has been the burden of a widespread spectrum of writing in contemporary biblical studies and theology that there are plenty of reasons for thinking that the tradition can be read in a more egalitarian way. One can find some evidence even in the Pauline passages just mentioned: Paul moderates his hierarchical scale by noting that 'in the Lord woman is not independent of man or man independent of woman . . . just as woman came from man, so man comes through woman . . . all things come from God' (1 Cor. 11.11–12). And the Ephesians 5 passage is prefaced by the striking notion of mutual subordination: 'be subject to one another out of reverence for Christ' (Eph. 5.21). Needless to say this has not been much observed in the Christian tradition either in theory or in practice, but even so it does point the way to a certain subversion of gender hierarchies. It intimates a *reciprocal* self-offering in relationship that makes extreme demands on the husband (up to self-sacrifice unto death: 'as Christ gave himself up for the church') as well as the wife. And in emphasizing what each partner can give to a relationship rather than what each may get from it, it has real attractions as a form of moral and pastoral advice which is likely to make for more successful marriages than those conducted on the basis of a rights-centred mentality. Nevertheless, even so, we should not forget that the husband is still analogized to Christ, the wife to the Church. The demands made on the husband can still be seen as a form of male condescension in a patriarchal society in which the man had to protect his property, including his wife: the image still implicitly reinforces the status quo. In other words, the idea of mutual subordination can only be finally secured from being a one-sided hierarchical subordination if it is clearly asserted that male and female are fundamentally, ontologically equal: it is quite possible, and compatible with other emphases in Paul, to assert mutual subordination within a fundamentally unequal framework in which the man is the head of the woman.

What must be affirmed instead is that mutual subordination must be located within a framework characterized by a basic equality and cannot be the grounding for that basic equality.

How that basic equality is to be ensured will to a certain extent be a matter of wider hermeneutical and theological commitments. Some might point to the relationship of the two creation narratives: even if the Genesis 2 account of the origins of Eve is not egalitarian, it is still nested within and subsequent to the apparent equality of Genesis 1.27, male and female in the image of God, which might be thought to take precedence because of its prominent literary position. Others might argue from the significance of the fundamental practices of the Church: for example, the sacrament of baptism in which no distinction is made between men and women, as established in the formula of Galatians 3.28 – there is no longer male and female, but all share a fundamental identity in Christ Jesus. Others again might cite Jesus' treatment of women by contrast with the conventions of the time, or the risen Lord's appearing first to women, or the Pentecostal experience of maidservants as well as menservants prophesying, or Paul's commitment to using women as co-workers in mission, all of which, together with many others, could be taken as evidence of the beginnings of the breakthrough of a different order.

The precise argument for a fundamental equality between men and women is less central to my concerns than what follows from the conclusion. For if one accepts as a legitimate reading of the overall biblical witness – despite some apparently plain biblical emphases to the contrary – that men and women are equal in Christ, and that it is proper for this to be reflected in gender relations now, then it follows that there is a case for rejecting gender subordination in marriage, and therefore that hierarchical order cannot be used as a conclusive argument for sexual differentiation in marriage. If both parties are to be regarded as ontologically equal, then the argument from hierarchy offers no grounds for rejecting same-sex marriage, since two partners of the same sex are by definition ontologically equal. If we are to hold that marriage must be heterosexual, we need to look elsewhere.

This brings us to a second kind of reason for thinking that marriage must be sexually differentiated, namely that it embodies an intrinsic complementarity that is not hierarchical, at least in principle. We should note that this last phrase does a lot of work, since it has been one of the central burdens of critical gender theory that binary oppositions always in practice privilege one of their elements: the logic of identity in Western thought ensures that in dichotomies such as mind/body, nature/culture, human/animal, subject/object, the identity of the first in each pair is secured by expelling or somehow problematizing the second. So also with the binary male/female. The ramifications of this are vast and various, and I am not going to explore them here: rather I will assume for the sake of argument that there could be non-hierarchical complementarity, in order to address the issue head on. My point will not be that putatively complementary, equal-but-different relationships can always be shown to be unequal in practice, but that even if non-hierarchical complementarity is indeed possible, the reasons for endorsing it would not be sufficient to reject same-sex relationships.

The argument takes at least three different forms, which I will outline before making a response.

The first of these is biological, or more precisely anatomical, in nature. Male and female genitalia are physically very precisely correlated to each other, and this suggests that human beings are physically suited for vaginal intercourse in a way that they are not for, say, anal intercourse. It only takes a little prompt about following the designs built into nature to deduce that sexual relations are intended by nature and nature's God to be heterosexual. Whether or not we are able to read very much of moral significance off nature, surely this at least is an example, the claim would go.

The second argument is based somewhere else entirely: instead of looking to biology, it looks to a variety of empirical or quasi-empirical claims from the human or social sciences to contend that the differences between men and women are so profound that the only kinds of sexual relationship that should be socially or legally recognized must be heterosexual. Women are better at understanding emotions, men at following abstract arguments;

women multi-task, men can only do one thing at a time; women ask for directions, men drive on. These may be pop psychological observations taken out of the *Men Are from Mars, Women Are from Venus* notebook, but the claims stretch with varying levels of applicability and plausibility from psychoanalysis to evolutionary psychology, from childhood and early developmental studies to criminology and the sociology of deviance, from sociolinguistics to cultural anthropology. Sexual difference is so pronounced and so marked, the thought goes, that it must be observed in such basic social institutions as marriage: in the Lord woman is not independent of man or man independent of woman, as the apostle maintains (1 Cor. 11.11). Another version of the claim, which likewise ultimately appeals to certain contingent generalizations about human sociality, argues quite properly that the well-being of society depends in part on the strength of its underlying structures, but then asserts that those structures must comprise families based on heterosexual marriage. Only if society is based on such a web of associations, dependent finally on the traditional, heterosexual family unit, can we be sure that it will hold together. Marriage 'enriches society and strengthens community', as the *Common Worship* marriage service declares; and in doing so it draws on an Anglican tradition that sees the family as the little commonwealth that provides for the common weal of the nation by nurturing its members in godly norms and habits.

The third argument for the necessary complementarity of marriage is purely theological in nature. On the basis of humankind being made in the image of God, Karl Barth maintains that the male–female encounter is intrinsic to all forms of human relating, including marriage. The triune God, he argues, is internally relational, and so creatures made in God's image must also be intrinsically beings-in-relation. But for human beings the element of sexual differentiation within this relationality is inescapable; the first time we meet human beings in Genesis, it is as male and female, and it is as male and female that they are made in the image of God. But Barth refuses to ground sexual differentiation in any general, specifiable feature of men and women: it is in the pure fact of encounter between them that they image God, however this is embodied, and not in any specific attribute such as a joint capacity for procreation, or differentiated gender roles, or psychological or other dissimilarities. It is not these differences but the male–female relationship as such which constitutes humanity fundamentally as humanity in relationship, since the difference of male and female is the primordial differentiation between human beings that is at the same time the 'one long reference to the relationship' between them.[2] Marriage constitutes one long reference to the relationship, and must inevitably be heterosexual.

All of these arguments are very lightly sketched, but they should still be adequate to allow us to discern the outlines of responses to them. The argument from anatomy, that tabs are made for some slots and not others, may have a certain intuitive appeal at least for some, since it seems to take the biological nature of human beings seriously, and that is essential for any theology that purports to have regard for creation. And in this respect it seems to parallel traditional Roman Catholic arguments about sexual intercourse, according to which the natural end of the female and male organs of reproduction is precisely reproduction. However, it is subtly and importantly different. As it stands, the argument from anatomy operates in separation from any account of what the reproductive organs are for; it appeals only to their anatomical shape and mutual physical fittedness, and neglects to note why they work together anatomically. In other words, it looks to their structure in abstraction from their function. But without an understanding of their function, namely reproduction, their structure is meaningless, just as a tangle of metalwork, cords and weights may fit well together but is meaningless until you realize that it makes up an exercise machine. The Catholic version of the argument is much preferable inasmuch as it talks of the natural end of intercourse, and so draws in the reproductive function from the start. The significance and problems of that approach,

---

2 Karl Barth, *Church Dogmatics*, III. 4: *The Doctrine of Creation* [1951], trans. A. T. MacKay et al., Edinburgh: T. & T. Clark, 1961, pp. 117–18.

however, we shall see later in the chapter when we come to the ethics of contraception.[3]

The second kind of argument for non-hierarchical complementarity appeals to a variety of contingent generalizations informed (or sometimes, one is tempted to think, *not* informed) by evidence from the various sciences. No doubt it may well be the case that many of these generalizations have a certain merit: perhaps in virtue of genetic endowment or intrauterine development or early childhood experience, male and female neurologies and psychologies tend to differ, rendering men more likely than women to display certain traits or behaviours, and vice versa. Maybe men and women do tend to have different structures of reasoning or emotion from each other. But then again, maybe not: who knows what findings next year's crop of research studies will deliver? Whatever merit such claims have is likely to be at the level of generalizations and provisional results. Even if it is the case that certain psychological generalizations of the men-read-maps-women-read-emotions variety do obtain, they remain generalizations, and typically do not obtain universally: some women read maps better than some men. But precisely because they have this provisional, contingent status, it is unclear how they can be theologically load-bearing. That is, it is unclear how they can provide the kind of *categorical* grounding that would be needed to make theological claims that permanent relationships *must* always be heterosexual in nature. The same applies to the argument from sociality. Even if it were the case that societies function best that are comprised of strong interrelating networks of heterosexual marriage-and-family structures, it requires another set of arguments to show that they are threatened more by unmarried same-sex couples wanting to enter into permanent

---

3 The 'pure anatomy' approach, in which the structure alone is thought to be capable of carrying moral significance, would consort well with some evangelical and Protestant efforts to defend simultaneously the morality of contraception and the immorality of same-sex relationships, since physical fittedness both legitimates some forms of penetrative sex while delegitimating others, and is unaffected by most contraceptive methods.

relationships than by, say, married heterosexual couples wanting to leave them.

It is surely for these kinds of reason that Barth refused to be drawn on any specifics about what the difference between male and female might consist in. The fact of encounter, not its particular empirical correlates, is what matters. However, it is not clear that his case for the necessary sexual differentiation of marriage fares any better. For once one has denied any specific grounding of difference (procreative capacity, psychological differences, or whatever), then one has lost any reason for thinking sexual differentiation is morally significant beyond the fact that it is 'commanded'. If it is the fact of encounter that is significant, why should that solely be between male and female? If it is the 'one long reference to relationship', that can only be because marriage must be for life; but then why should that marriage be of an opposite-sex couple? Ultimately, the only difference Barth can point to is that of a certain 'precedence' on the part of the man and 'subsequence' on the part of the woman. But this suggests that the distinction can only be sustained by recourse to the hierarchical version of complementarity I referred to earlier, which in turns fuels the suspicions of those who were never inclined to be sympathetic towards complementarian schemes in the first place. Although the overall structure of Barth's theology of the sexes is arguably more egalitarian in initial inspiration, which is why I discuss it here rather than as a form of hierarchical complementarity, it seems in the end unable to hide its secret inequality-in-difference.

Perhaps even more decisive than these points is that Barth surely misinterprets the actual ground given in Genesis 1 for sexual differentiation, namely the role that it plays in procreation. And this leads us on to the third kind of argument given in the Christian tradition for sexual differentiation in marriage, namely that marriage in creation is intrinsically procreative. As we saw in Chapter 1, the significance of being created male and female in Genesis 1 is not that humankind thereby images the inner relationality of God, but that sexual differentiation is the necessary basis for human beings to procreate. To be in the image of God is to have a mandate to rule on God's behalf, and that rule is enabled by having

47

children: by being fruitful and multiplying, humankind is thereby able to fill the earth, subdue it and have stewardship of the other creatures. In other words, the reason for there being two sexes is that this is the way the human species reproduces. Children might in the divine providence have come to be by means other than sex: they could have been produced by some asexual self-propagation of a single-sex species. But in the world with which we have to do they come to be as the fruit of a couple's relationship; and that is not just adventitious, as if the parents' one-flesh union were one thing and the child's coming to be something entirely other. Rather for a couple to experience the miracle of procreation as a fruit of their mutual love is also for them to come to know something of the miracle of creation itself as the free outpouring of the divine love.

If we are to understand marriage in creation as therefore intrinsically heterosexual, it is not because it fits a complementarian scheme, hierarchical or non-hierarchical, but because it is intrinsically open to procreation. Augustine once remarked that if marriage were for companionship, then God would surely have created another man to be with Adam. While the comment may tell us something about Augustine's attitude to women, it also shows us that without procreation the reasons for sexual differentiation become moot. But the association of sexual differentiation with procreation is not just a theological claim. It is also biologically the case that human reproduction does require both male and female, a fact whose ramifications have been drawn out in extraordinary detail in evolutionary biology. And beyond that, as a general claim about the history and evolution of human cultures, it is not implausible to trace the ultimate cause of gender difference overwhelmingly to the different roles men and women play in relation to the conception, gestation and upbringing of children. Gender complementarity in other words is itself very significantly predicated on the connection of sexual differentiation with procreation.

Sexual differentiation is therefore justified within marriage, but it is only justified because marriage in creation is oriented to procreation. There are no other grounds that can provide the theological weight needed to *require* that marriage be sexually differentiated. However, this also implies that if procreation is no longer eschatologically necessary, then there are no grounds for requiring all committed relationships to be heterosexual. If there is a theological case for eschatologically grounded covenant partnerships which are inherently non-procreative, there is no reason why they should be heterosexual. Indeed Augustine recognized the logic of the position. He accepted that there would be two sexes in heaven, but struggled to understand what rationale sexual differentiation would continue to have, speculating that through appreciation of the beauty of the other sex we would be moved to praise God the more. And we may find the beginnings of such a recognition in the writings of Paul himself. In his celebrated formula in Galatians 3.28, he strikingly writes that in Christ 'there is no longer Jew or Greek . . . no longer slave or free . . . no longer male *and* female': where we might have expected the parallel 'male or female', he appears instead deliberately to echo Genesis 1.27 ('male and female he created them'). Baptism and the new identity in Christ take us beyond the creation categories of male and female in a way that renders them no longer of defining importance.

Indeed, teasingly, we may even find the creation categories here partly contradicted, opening up among other things the possibility that those who do not find their bodies easily mapping on to the creation duality might find their identity in Christ. Clearly this is of decisive significance for thinking about intersex conditions and disorders of sex development more generally: to find one's identity in Christ does not mean having to be conformed to one side or another of a biological binary. But it also underlines a central implication that emerges out of the idea of covenant partnerships. If they are defined as non-procreative, and if sexual differentiation is unnecessary for them, they are open to all: whatever one's place on the spectrum of sexual differentiation, whatever one's gender identity, whatever one's sexual orientation, whatever one's capacity or lack of capacity for procreation, the fundamental question is of calling to covenant partnership. The issue is not one's physiology or the direction of one's desires, but the willingness to commit to a particular person, with a view to faithfulness, permanence, and fruitfulness. Finding oneself in Christ does not mean the dissolution of all other identities, but rather submitting them to Christ and being open to the calling to witness to God's covenant faithfulness, in the sanctifying reality of a particular relationship.

If none of the arguments for the necessity of sexual differentiation work, we can look to a picture of the Church in which different people have different callings. Some are called to marriage that is open to procreation to show forth God's continuing commitment to his creation. Some are called to celibacy to point forward to the time when God will be all in all. And some are called to non-procreative covenant relationships to witness to the time between the times, when God's purposes for creation have been fulfilled in Christ, but where we await their final manifestation. But all have a gifting within the Church, and all are called to discern their gifting.[4]

Covenant partnerships and sex

Up to this point in arguing for covenant partnerships I have presumed that they will be expressed sexually. However, someone who wanted to defend traditional Christian teaching on same-sex relationships might respond that they would be quite happy wholly to endorse the notion of covenant partnerships, but with the proviso that such relationships should be non-sexual. After all, the Bible does indeed know of sworn, covenanted same-sex relationships – David and Jonathan being the most obvious of these – but there is no reason to assume from the biblical text or from the historical context that these would have been sexual in

---

4 Although I have not pursued the possibility here, the idea of non-vowed singleness as another kind of calling is found in Victor Preller, 'Sexual Ethics and the Single Life', in Philip Turner (ed.), *Men and Women: Sexual Ethics in Turbulent Times*, Cambridge, MA: Cowley Publications, 1989, pp. 116–46.

nature; and so, the argument would go, they provide no biblical precedent for sexually expressed covenant partnership.

It is no part of my argument to claim that the relationship of David and Jonathan – or those of Ruth and Naomi, or of Jesus and the beloved disciple – were sexual. They were clearly charged with a wonderful intensity of affection, but the case for suggesting that any of them were genitally expressed has to contend not only with the silence of the texts on the matter but also with the tidal flow of cultural expectations in the opposite direction. The argument for covenant partnerships proposed here is based not on speculations about biblical examples of homosocial attachments, but on thinking through the significance of New Testament eschatology for procreation; and it applies to heterosexual as much as to homosexual relationships. However, the probability that the biblical examples were not genitally sexual still leaves us with the question whether covenant partnerships in the sense proposed here may indeed be sexual and what the meaning of sexuality within them might be.

Before addressing the issue directly, let me make two observations. The first concerns the place in which this question comes in the argument. As I present it, the shape of the question is not in the first place about sex, but about relationships. That is, the first question we should ask is not about who you may have sex with and when, or about how far you can go, but about what kinds of relationships we should be committed to. Sex does not exist as a free-floating entity independent of relationship, but gains its meaning from the relationship to which it belongs and which forms its context. An ethics of sex therefore does not start off from reflections on the nature of sex, but from thinking about relationship: the questions of who one is committed to and what the meaning of that commitment is form the setting against which to think about what one may do within that relationship.

Affirming that sex is set in relationship, and that it is the latter that is the primary object of moral enquiry, does not imply that the meaning of sex is whatever the couple decide to make it mean, as we shall see in a moment when we look at the ethics of contraception. But it does relegate to a secondary position a series of detailed questions about what counts as sex. If we talk of 'the act of sex' or 'the marital act', are we only referring to vaginal intercourse? In male same-sex relations, do we only mean anal intercourse? What about heterosexual anal intercourse? What does 'the sexual act' mean for lesbians? What about foreplay? Or mutual masturbation? Or oral sex? Or different sex positions? Or sex toys? Or the infliction or acceptance of pain as part of sexual pleasure? It may be no surprise to hear that the Bible does not on the whole address itself to these kinds of questions, except on particularly adventurous readings; while it is possible to specu-late on the reasons for its silence in particular cases, at least one reason is that, in its concern that sex should symbolize God's holi-ness, it is directed more to the question of who we have sexual relations with than what those sexual relations might consist in.

The second observation concerns the differences between this account of covenant partnerships and defences of same-sex rela-tionships that see them as a form of friendship. Certainly there are similarities between the covenant partnership model and the friendship model. Notably, both of them agree that marriage can-not be taken unproblematically as the framework within which to understand same-sex relationships. Covenant partnership and friendship are also connected in that at a formal level they are both species of which friendship *in its broadest sense* is the genus; just as marriage also is a species of friendship in this broader sense. Moreover, the notion of friendship has a noble history in the tradition of Christian theology: among many other places in which it recurs, for Aquinas friendship names our relationship with God, such that to be saved is to be made capable of friend-ship. Indeed considerations of this sort suggest the attractiveness of the language of 'covenant friendship' in addition to or even instead of 'covenant partnership'.

However, there are also good reasons for taking care about turning to the language of friendship. In the modern West, friend-ship suggests a less well-defined relationship than permanent com-mitment. There are no clearly marked distinctions between being a friend, on the one hand, and being merely an acquaintance or a colleague or someone who hangs around in the same social group, on the other. Friendship ordinarily connotes a non-sexual relationship: when we say that two people are 'just friends', we imply that their relationship is non-romantic and non-erotic. Faithful may be the wounds of a friend, but friendships also come and go. 'Call no one a friend until you have eaten a pound of salt with them', says a Russian proverb, but, however elevated and attractive the sentiment, the difference between that and a Facebook friend one has never met and will never meet is finally a matter of degree rather than of kind. By contrast, a formally celebrated and publicly recognized undertaking of marriage or covenant partnership indicates entry into a set of commitments that is different in kind and brings with it definable and perhaps legally enforceable rights and obligations. Of course in marriages or covenant partnerships the partners may well be the best of friends, and it is wonderful when they are; and of course in a formal sense marriages and covenant partnerships are both species of friendship in the more generic sense. But they remain categorically different from friendships in the conventional contemporary usage of the term.

In other words it is one specifiable kind of friendship that is of concern here, namely friendship that is characterized by publicly vowed commitments to faithfulness, permanence, and openness to procreation (in the case of marriage) or fruitfulness (in the case of covenant partnership). To model same-sex relationships on friendship in its everyday sense runs the risk of imbuing them with the qualities of open-endedness and non-exclusiveness, which are the peculiar glories of friendship and ensure its irreplaceable role in the catalogue of possible social relationships, but are also precisely not what committed partnerships are called to display. And in using the language of friendship, despite its very best intentions, this model may again ironically reinforce the sense that same-sex relationships are irretrievably second class: it is in danger of reinscribing subliminal – or not so subliminal – cultural messages of outsider status, that lesbian and gay people will never be quite able to attain what is conventionally taken to be the gold standard of human relations, namely marriage. Whether covenant partnerships court the same difficulty is a question we will return to in Chapter 5.

Affirming that sex is always to be understood in the context of relationship still leaves room for a category of non-sexually expressed friendships and partnerships. I earlier argued for a revitalization of the calling to celibacy, but of course celibacy is not the same as singleness. Since the early centuries of the Church's history there have always been anchorites, hermits and other celibates who have been called to the solitary life in partial or total separation from others, but the majority of those who have taken vows of celibacy have done so in the context of a shared life: coenobitic or communally based religious orders, whose members submit to a common discipline, have been the predominant context in which celibacy has been lived out. A renewal of such communities, some connected with the founding of new religious orders, others drawing on and sustained by the discipline of already existing orders, whether long-standing or more recent, would be one readily conceivable way in which the vocation to celibacy might be refreshed. The renewal of communal celibacy is happening in some places and it might be complemented by proposals for exploring celibate spiritual friendships and the like that are also being actively explored in some quarters. We live in times that are pregnant with possibility: all of these are forms of life that deserve to be considered more fully, and the idea of a calling to celibate covenant partnership should certainly be included among them – albeit without forgetting familiar lessons about the dangers of 'particular friendships' in the religious life.

However, might it not also be that not all who are called to covenant partnership are also called to celibacy? Could covenant partnerships indeed be sexually expressed? To investigate this we need to think through the nature and purposes of sex. So far we have only considered sex in the context of marriage, in relation to its role in procreation. Marriage as a creation ordinance is inextricably linked to procreation, I argued earlier: its procreativity is one of the three goods which conjointly make it distinct from all other kinds of human relationship. Yet even if *marriage* is unavoidably linked to procreation, does it follow that *sex* is also unavoidably linked to procreation? If it does follow, it would imply that every time a married couple has sex, they must be open to the possibility of having children. Even if sex additionally and simultaneously has other roles in a couple's relationship, it would always have to have that procreative possibility.

If we turn to the Bible to address this issue, there are some hints that sex has roles other than procreation. Paul talks about sex in a way that suggests that the connection between sex and having children was not at the top of his mind: the husband 'should give to his wife her conjugal rights, and likewise the wife to her husband' (1 Cor. 7.3). Indeed, the connection with having children is not unambiguously mentioned at any point in the passage. While it might be claimed that one's 'conjugal rights' (*hē opheilē*) refer to the opportunity for having children, Paul sets his discussion in the context of marriage being needed because of cases of sexual immorality (7.2) and of the partners not depriving each other except by agreement for set times for the sake of prayer (7.5); and this suggests that he is talking about exactly what we moderns would naturally imagine when reading it, namely having sex for its own sake rather than for the sake of having children.

There are also other passages that imply or suggest sexual love without clear reference to procreativity: the Genesis 2 account of the man and woman becoming one flesh comes to mind, for example, or the gorgeous erotic poetry of the Song of Songs. These may all arguably be taken as evidence that erotic desire and its sexual expression are a good, even outside of the context of having children. Nevertheless, on the other hand, it might be replied that at no point are any of the biblical authors deliberately excluding the possibility of children: after all, without reliable contraception the connection between sex and procreativity was one of the givens of life, so wholly taken for granted that it did not occur to them to comment explicitly on the matter. In other words, even if sex rightly has many meanings in a couple's life apart from being the means by which they may have children, it might be that the Bible never countenances the possibility of sex without procreative potential.

We cannot avoid turning to broader considerations about the ethics of contraception, therefore. It remains the Roman Catholic Church's official teaching that artificial contraceptive techniques are intrinsically wrong: 'each and every marriage act must remain open to the transmission of life', declared *Humanae Vitae*, Paul VI's 1968 encyclical which reaffirmed the traditional Catholic teaching. This doctrine, the encyclical continued, 'is based on the inseparable connection, established by God, which man on his own initiative may not break, between the unitive significance and the procreative significance which are both inherent to the marriage act' (*Humanae Vitae*, para. 12). Married love tends of itself to be fruitful, and the unitive significance of sex (its tendency to foster the partners' love for each other) cannot be separated from its procreative significance.

There have been many interpretations and defences of this teaching. One more traditional understanding appeals to a 'perverted faculty' argument, that contraception frustrates the natural biological end of sex. Although elements of this approach are still important, as we shall see, it is regularly and rightly criticized for reducing the integral unity of the personal and physical encounter to a merely biological transaction: to be a human being is after all to be more than a biological being, and to object to contraception on this ground alone would also raise questions about any kind of intervention in the body's biological rhythms, from shaving and cutting one's nails to many kinds of medical treatment. It must make *some* difference to our understanding of human sexual relations that we are personal and cultural beings, even if it remains to be determined exactly what that difference is.

Much more intriguing and substantial is the argument offered by Pope John Paul II, both when he was Pope and previously as Karol Wojtyla.[5] His fundamental concern is not that contraception deprives sex of its biological potential, but that it deprives sex of its personal meaning. Human nature is indeed integrated in the person and not just in the biological body. This means that the physical act cannot be separated from the person. But it equally also means that the person cannot be separated from the physical

---

5 John Paul II, *Man and Woman He Created Them: A Theology of the Body*, trans. Michael Waldstein, Boston, MA: Pauline Books and Media, 2006.

act: if sex is truly to be an act of personal communion, he maintains, it cannot just consist in the disembodied relationality of two lovers, but must involve the total self-giving of each of the partners, including the gift by each of their capacity for fertility. Contraception denies that self-gift and refuses the self-gift of the other by refusing their gift of fertility. It is therefore a denial of love, which involves the giving of the whole self and not just one dimension of the self; love, one might say, is inherently procreative. John Paul II is very clear that love here is intended in an objective sense: subjectively, in terms of the felt emotions of the couple, contracepted sex can be very loving, but objectively it should in fact be seen as a denial of love. In this respect he goes beyond earlier teachings, which maintained that the unitive and procreative ends of sex should not be separated, but which nevertheless allowed that contracepted sex could be loving in an objective sense and therefore could at least embody the unitive end; for him, the unitive end of embodying and fostering the couple's love is fundamentally violated and denied by contraception – the marital act in such circumstances is not a personal union, but becomes a mere 'sexual association'.

There is undoubtedly a grandeur in John Paul II's vision, in its rejection of both physicalist reduction and subjectivist relationality, and its refusal to deny the physical even as he integrates it into his account of the personal. Nevertheless, it is one thing to acknowledge these features, another to accept his account in its entirety. Historically, one of the main lines of criticism among Roman Catholic moral theologians has been that contraception can be justified by the good of the marriage as a whole and the good that the marriage serves: among other things, contraception allows a couple to nurture each other in love and to bring up a family without fear that the quality of attention (not to speak of the amount of the family budget) that can be devoted to each of their children will be jeopardized by the number of children they have. But such a defence always runs the danger of seeming to appeal to the good of the marriage as a whole in order to justify a contraceptive practice that is tacitly admitted to be inherently morally problematic. What we need to affirm instead is that the primary unit for moral consideration is not the individual 'marital act', but the marriage itself as a whole. It is not particular sexual acts that bear the moral weight in the first place, but the entirety of the relationship that forms their context. The personal union of a married couple has an intrinsic temporal dimension that stretches across the lifetime of their marriage; as Oliver O'Donovan has written, marriage should not be conceptualized in a way that reduces it to a series of one-night stands.[6] Instead we should insist, as I argued earlier, that sex gains its meaning inseparably from the relational context in which it is set. This does not mean that meaning provided by the context necessarily trumps all other possible meanings of individual sexual encounters: marital rape is not the less rape for taking place within a marriage. But it does suggest that procreativity is properly predicated of marriage as a whole, not of particular occasions of sexual intimacy. And if this is so, even if marriage itself must always be open to new life, it does not follow that contraception as such is always wrong.

The Roman Catholic discussion has of course been much more ramified and complex than is evident from these comments. But if we return to the question that gave rise to it, the point remains: however one reaches the conclusion, if one concedes that contraception is justifiable, one also concedes that sex is characterized by a good which is independent of and additional to its orientation to procreation.

We should note that it does not immediately follow from accepting the morality of contraception that same-sex sexual relationships are also justified. All that follows from endorsing contraception is that sex has other roles and is open to other meanings and purposes than procreation; it would be quite possible to argue that the only appropriate context of sex remains that of heterosexual marriage. Nor does it follow that once sex is separated from a necessary connection with procreation, it is morally acceptable in any context whatsoever, however casual, fleeting,

---

6 Oliver O'Donovan, *Resurrection and Moral Order*, second edition, Leicester: InterVarsity Press, 1994, p. 210.

pecuniary, exploitative, predatory or coercive that context may be; on the contrary, sex still takes its primary moral bearings from the relationship it is – or fails to be – a part of.

What opens the path to affirming sexual same-sex relationships is rather, first, determining what kinds of relationships we are called to be committed to, whether marriage alone or, as I have argued, also eschatologically grounded covenant partnerships that are not procreative in nature; and then establishing the claim that there is no necessary complementarity between the sexes other than that of procreation; and then putting those arguments together, the conclusion that covenant partnerships may be same-sex in nature. Only when we have established the nature of the relationships that form the context can we turn to the question of whether sex may or may not take place within them and what the meaning of that sex might be. To then accept that contraception is in principle legitimate is to admit that sex may have, intrinsically and objectively and not just in the choices or willings of the partners, a different and separable meaning from procreativity. And this in turn implies that covenant partnerships, whether heterosexual or homosexual, may be sexual in nature.

What does the non-procreative good of sex consist in? A detailed account of this would need to be unfurled out of the formal moral theological category of the unitive end into a much fuller display. There is no shortage of contemporary writers on sex, theological and non-theological, who have addressed themselves to this – though strangely most of them seem to be entirely untroubled by not having the formal moral theological vocabulary to draw upon.

Here I will mention only the connection between sexual intimacy and our knowledge of God. We saw earlier that both marriage and covenant partnerships witness to the covenant relationship between God and God's people, in that they are both called to reflect the permanence and faithfulness of God's self-commitment. Likewise, sex embodies and points to the nature of our relationship with God. The Song of Songs is included in the canon no doubt in part because of the allegorical readings to which it lent itself: Bernard of Clairvaux's sermons on them stand as the most prominent of many such examples, interpreting the bridegroom as Christ and the bride as the Church or as the individual before God. To be desired by another whom you yourself desire, to know that you are a joy for another who is in turn a joy for you, these are at the heart of erotic and so of sexual encounter: the intimacy of communion that one experiences with another is a foretaste of the intimacy of communion one will experience with God. Sexual relationship may thus become a glimpse into the inner life of God and focus for us the very reason for our creation, that we might participate in this. As Rowan Williams memorably writes:

> The whole story of creation, incarnation and our redemption into the fellowship of Christ's body tells us that God desires us, *as if we were God*, as if we were that unconditional response to God's giving that God's self makes in the life of the Trinity. We are created so that we may be caught up in this; so that we may grow into the wholehearted love of God by learning that God loves us as God loves God.[7]

And yet if sex does point us towards God's love of God, it also does so by pointing beyond itself. It is a creaturely symbol and as such never carries the fullness in itself: erotic desire fades, sexual ecstasy is a moment's pleasure. It may provide a sense of fulfilment for a while, but it always leaves one longing for something more. Without that sense of pointing beyond itself, it is always in danger of becoming an idol; with that sense, it can become an icon of the divine love.

Our erotic desire for God, and of God for us, and of God for God, is not only intimated to us through the medium of genitally expressed sexuality, of course: such is the witness of celibate mystics down the ages, whose expressions of the desire of God demonstrate an erotic intensity in comparison with which

---

7 Rowan Williams, 'The Body's Grace', in Eugene F. Rogers Jr (ed.), *Theology and Sexuality: Classic and Contemporary Readings*, Oxford: Blackwell, 2002, pp. 309–21, at pp. 311–12 (italics amended).

most everyday sexual relationships pale. But for us as embodied beings with the bodies we have in this life, sexual, genital relationship is an entirely appropriate form of expression. We do not know what form our bodies will take in the life to come: Paul rounded on those who speculated on the nature of the resurrection body with a single word, 'Fool!' (1 Cor. 15.36). Nor, beyond there being neither marrying nor giving in marriage, do we know what form human intimacy could take in a time when we will no longer see through a glass darkly but will see Love face to face. If the life hereafter is without sex in any sense with which we are acquainted, it will not be because it will be less than the sex we are familiar with, but because it will be more: there is a difference, as C. S. Lewis remarked, between nonsensuousness and trans-sensuousness.[8] But for us, here and now, eroticized bodily touch is a wholly apposite expression of our embodiedness and of our unreserved self-giving to one another. To touch, to hold, to feel, to need: the vulnerability of baring one's body to another, of being fully known by another and yet of being fully accepted by that other, and of rendering that love in return, can indeed make sexual intimacy a participation in divine grace. And as the Song of Songs itself may be taken to imply, it is precisely as sexual, embodied beings that we may find ourselves being drawn towards the source of all love.

---

8 C. S. Lewis, *Perelandra* [1944], New York: Scribner, 2003, p. 30. Cf. Ransom's expostulation that to describe it as sexless is 'about as good a description of living in Perelandra as it would be to say that a man had forgotten water because Niagara Falls didn't immediately give him the idea of making it into cups of tea' (ibid., p. 76).

4

Reading the Bible

'Congratulations to those of you who have turned to this chapter first!' So began the chapter on sex in a book on marriage given to intending couples at marriage preparation classes. And congratulations also to those who have turned to this chapter first; it says something when in a book on sex the first place some readers will turn to is the chapter on the Bible. I have of course been endeavouring to interpret Scripture throughout, attempting to draw on Scripture for theological purposes. Whether this particular effort is successful or not is a matter for the reader to decide, but we do have to shake off the assumption that pervades swathes of discussion on Christian ethics and homosexuality that the primary task is to reiterate – or attempt to get round – the half-dozen or so biblical texts that appear to refer directly to same-sex relations. I have left discussion of these deliberately late, since we need to understand the basic scriptural and theological shape of the issues first before we will be able to locate these particular texts appropriately. It is sometimes said that the Bible's teachings on same-sex relationships could be discerned even if none of these verses had been written. I am tempted to agree, even if I am inclined to rather different conclusions from those who usually make the claim.

Nothing I am going to say depends on radically novel or unconventional exegeses of individual texts. I am prepared to accept for the sake of argument that whatever it was that the biblical writers were referring to in relation to same-sex sexuality, they took themselves to be opposed to it. Of course what they were opposed to, and how that maps on to our own categories, is a less straightforward thing to decide, as plenty of recent discussion has shown.

But even here my argument is not going to depend on unusually picky subtleties: do we really have to make much of the fact that Leviticus only explicitly mentions lying with a male 'as with a woman', and that this might leave some room for male same-sex relations that are non-penetrative? Or that Romans 1 allegedly does not explicitly condemn lesbian behaviour but only lesbian passions? Rather I want to let the overall story and the picture it gives us about life lived between the times of the resurrection and the *parousia* set the pace, and interpret particular texts in the light of that.

We are faced therefore not so much with a choice of either following 'the plain meaning of Scripture' on the one hand or plain disobedience on the other, as of drawing a contrast between the surface meaning of texts and the deeper structure of the biblical story. It is this deeper story that I have sought to elaborate in the past three chapters, looking at creation, covenant, Christ, resurrection, eschatology and ecclesiology, and then at the biblical understanding of man and woman, sex, marriage and children in the light of these. Of course an exploration of these themes does not simply trump or bulldoze recalcitrant verses that do not fit: the task of interpreting Scripture is a dance, disciplined but also free, of referring backwards and forwards between the particular and the general, and different interpreters will take different views on where and how the balance is best struck between these. But wherever and however one decides to strike that balance, a balance there must be.

Romans 1

How then are we to interpret the biblical texts that do appear to address questions of same-sex sexuality? I want to start with Romans 1.18–32, which is widely agreed to be the most significant of all the texts. This is in part because of the pivotal position it occupies in the letter to the Romans, which is itself the most extended statement of Paul's theology. It is also in part because Paul here gives it a deep theological and ontological grounding; the condemnation of same-sex relations does not appear incidental – unlike the other texts it is not a story with questionable moral significance, nor one of a seemingly arbitrary list of prohibitions, nor an item in a debatable catalogue of vices, but is given an extended rationale. But it is also because it sums up many of the concerns expressed in the other verses.

The passage is part of a longer argument that stretches from 1.18 to 3.20, in which Paul is arguing that all have sinned, both Jew and Gentile alike, and therefore are in need of the salvation that is proclaimed in the gospel. The wrath of God has been revealed, he declares, against all those who through their wickedness suppress the knowledge of God and his ways. Although God's nature can be plainly discerned through his creation, humankind has refused to honour God or be grateful to him, and so their minds have become darkened. Despite their professed wisdom, they have chosen to worship idols rather than the immortal God. As a result,

> [24]God gave them up in the lusts of their hearts to impurity, to the degrading of their bodies among themselves . . . [26]God gave them up to degrading passions. Their women exchanged natural intercourse for unnatural, [27]and in the same way also the men, giving up natural intercourse with women, were consumed with passion for one another. Men committed shameless acts with men and received in their own persons the due penalty for their error. (Rom. 1.24–27)

And since they chose not to acknowledge God, Paul continues, God has given them up to a debased mind and to every kind of wickedness.

It is not entirely clear who Paul is addressing at this stage in the letter. It is conventionally regarded as being addressed to Jewish readers: it has strong similarities to anti-Gentile diatribes of the time, and it is usually thought that Paul is leaning on these in order to draw readers in to join in the condemnation, only for Paul to turn on them and expose their hypocrisy: 'you have no excuse, whoever you are, when you judge others; for in passing judgement on another you condemn yourself, because you, the judge, are doing the very same things' (2.1). But the text is not that explicit; while he is clearly addressing the Jewish reader by

2.17, other scholars argue that the phrase 'whoever you are' suggests that Paul is addressing all human beings as such. However, for our purposes it does not matter too much. For the decisive thing to note about the passage is that it is set against the context of an understanding of creation and its relation to the law. Gentiles who do not have the law nevertheless know by nature what the law requires (2.14); those who have sinned under the law will be judged by the law, while those who sin apart from the law will also perish apart from the law (2.12). There is a law in creation that is reflected in the law given to the Jews; or perhaps better, there is a law given to the Jews that is also known through creation by those to whom the law has not been given, since it is the same God who has given both.

This connection between the law given to the Jews and the order of creation gives us the basic orientation for interpreting this passage. There are many texts that have been proposed as having influenced Paul's writing on same-sex relations. Among the most plausible are Wisdom 11–15 on the turning away by Gentiles from the true God to the worship of idols, with consequences in terms of sexual immorality ('the idea of making idols was the beginning of sexual immorality' (14.12)), and the Leviticus verses (18.22; 20.13) prohibiting men from lying with men as with a woman. But surely pre-eminent among them must be Paul's reading of Genesis 1 and his understanding of what happens when the creation order is reversed as a result of human sinfulness. As we have seen, the Genesis narrative tells of humankind being made in the image of God and being blessed and commanded to be fruitful and multiply, to subdue the earth and to have dominion over the fish of the sea, the birds of the air and every living thing that moves upon the earth; and critical to being able to be fruitful and multiply is that human beings are made male and female. We are given, in other words, a straightforward picture of a hierarchy of being, with God as supreme, sexually differentiated human beings made in his image below him, and animals in turn below them.

As a result of human fallenness (and we do not need to deliberate whether this is due to a primeval fall on the part of Adam or a subsequent fall due to idolatry), this creation ordering is reversed. It is this reversal that explains some of the more unusual features of this passage. Instead of worshipping God, who can be known through nature, human beings suppress the truth. Instead of worshipping God who is above them, human beings turn to worshipping the creatures that are below them. The idols that they worship are identified because they are either human but not divine or they are the kinds of creatures that should be recognizing human rule according to Genesis 1.28, not because as a matter of empirical observation Gentiles were especially given to worshipping birds or four-footed animals or reptiles. And instead of being fruitful and multiplying in their sexually differentiated and procreative rule over the earth, they instead burn with desire for each other, women turning to women and men to men. Again it is because Paul is reading Genesis 1 that he mentions lesbian relations, uniquely in the Old and New Testaments and unusually for the time as for all other times, not because he was commenting on its prevalence in Greco-Roman society, but simply because it follows from the reversal of Genesis 1.27.

It is this inversion of the Genesis account that is the key to understanding the passage. There is even a possibility that he is implicitly referring to the connection between sexual differentiation and procreation in this passage. Paul writes that men receive in their own persons (*en heautois*, literally 'in themselves') the penalty for same-sex relations (1.27), which has caused much perplexity among commentators. Some think that he is claiming that homosexuality is its own penalty (by parallel with the old vaudeville joke, 'What is the punishment for bigamy? Answer: Two wives'). Others speculate that the penalty might be feminization (as the implication of being penetrated), or sexually transmitted disease, or a waste in money or time, or even physical soreness. Aside from their other inadequacies, the term *bathos* is scarcely adequate to most of these suggestions, as if the whole wrath of God has been revealed against human beings for having suppressed the knowledge of God, and the penalty is . . . minor physical pain! By comparison, those interpretations that see the penalty as death, by parallel with the death that is the penalty of other vices (1.32), at least give a more adequate account of the scale of the sin. But much better, surely, is the interpretation that childlessness, as the entirely apt consequence of same-sex relations, is the punishment; when the command to be fruitful and multiply, which depends on sexual differentiation, is rejected, the natural corollary of non-procreative sex is non-procreation. In other words, in rejecting same-sex relations Paul's argument turns not on a conception of sexual complementarity which can be abstracted from procreation, but on the connection between sexual differentiation and procreation.

What Paul is providing here is an account of a fall from the created, protological good. And this is exactly what we would expect at this point in his argument. Since creation is understood in terms of procreative, sexually differentiated order, a fall from it would be portrayed in terms of a disruption of that order. But what he is *not* doing is providing a complete, considered sexual ethic. In particular, he is not at all addressing the question whether there might be any other way of understanding same-sex relations than a departure from a creation good. Of course, one can see a case for saying that homosexual attraction is against created norms, and this is what the historic theological case has rested on. But as I have tried to sketch out in the earlier chapters of this book, that is not at all the same as saying that this is the sum of what Christian theology might have to say on the matter, all things considered. Paul's argument at this point does not depend on explicit knowledge of Christ, but only on what people know in creation independently of Christ, the Gentiles without the law, the Jews with it. But if Christ's coming is decisive for our understanding of marriage and sexuality, as I have argued that it is, then there is more to be said, and more than the rhetorical stage in the argument could have allowed Paul to say.

Other biblical texts

This is not to say that Paul himself would have said something different, of course, but even if he did not reach the conclusions we have explored above, it should not prevent us from attending to the logic both of his thought and that of the New Testament as a whole. But before we return to these questions we should consider some of the other biblical texts, all of which turn, to the extent to which they carry force, on this same creation patterning.

In the story of Sodom in Genesis 19, two angelic visitors are offered hospitality by Lot, but the men of Sodom surround Lot's house and demand to 'know' his visitors. Lot refuses to let them in and offers instead his two daughters who have not known a man. The men of Sodom are not pacified by this, but are struck blind by the angels, and the whole of Sodom is destroyed in a rain of fire and sulphur. It is a brutal story of attempted homosexual gang rape, worsened by the implied status of daughters as their father's property. However, ever since Derrick Sherwin Bailey, writing in the 1950s, the story of Sodom has frequently been understood to refer to the sin of inhospitality rather than to the sin to which it has given its name.[1] And there is something to be said in favour of this. Apart from the varying understandings of the sin of Sodom found elsewhere in Scripture (e.g. Ezek. 16.49–50, according to which Sodom had 'pride, excesses of food, and prosperous ease, but did not aid the poor and needy'), Lot counters the men of Sodom by pleading that they do nothing to the visitors, 'for they have come under the shelter of my roof' (Gen. 19.8); it is better to offer his daughters, with all that would entail for their future unmarriageability, than for him to be inhospitable. Telling also is the difference between the reception the angels receive in Sodom and the gracious hospitality that they receive from Abraham and Sarah in the previous chapter; the contrastive parallelism of the two stories is striking. On the other hand, however, to say that the sin was not sexual at all seems unlikely. Among other things, it seems implausible that the 'knowledge' the men of Sodom demand of Lot's guests in verse 5 is different from the clearly sexual knowledge that we are told Lot's daughters have not experienced, two verses later.

However we are to interpret the Sodom passage, a story of violent homosexual gang rape is scarcely a secure basis from which

---

1 Derrick Sherwin Bailey, *Homosexuality and the Western Christian Tradition*, London: Longmans, 1955.

to construct an ethic of consensual, faithful and permanent same-sex partnerships. A similar conclusion, though for different reasons, has often been drawn from the two verses in Leviticus we have already referred to. 'You shall not lie with a male as with a woman; it is an abomination' (Lev. 18.22). 'If a man lies with a male as with a woman, both of them have committed an abomination; they shall be put to death; their blood is upon them' (Lev. 20.13). These verses come from the so-called Holiness Code of Leviticus 17—26, a list of prohibitions and prescriptions governing every area of Israel's life, including not least sexual behaviour. It seems difficult on the face of it to see these as referring to something other than homosexual anal intercourse, and much of the debate has focused not on what they refer to so much as why they pick out this particular behaviour, especially because it is specifically described as an 'abomination'. Although attempts have been made to understand the basis of the prohibition by claims that, for example, it refers to sexual relations in a non-Israelite cultic context, the most plausible interpretations relate it to that which unites many or perhaps all the sexual prohibitions in Leviticus, namely a purity code grounded in the preservation and stability of heterosexual marriage with procreation. That is, the prohibition is grounded in the vision of human sexuality that we find in Genesis 1.

One response to the Leviticus texts has been to argue that they are no longer binding on Christians, since according to the Christian hermeneutic of Old Testament law (reflected in, for example, Article 7 of the Church of England's 39 Articles) the ritual purity laws have been fulfilled in Christ and are therefore no longer binding on Christians, unlike the moral laws, which still hold. We no longer take the verses as binding that prohibit a man from having sex with a woman during her period (Lev. 18.19), nor do we follow the dietary laws or the laws against mixing of kinds. The laws against same-sex behaviour should similarly be jettisoned, the argument would go.

However, the argument is a little too quick. The task for the Christian interpreter is not simply to throw out the Levitical laws as a whole, but rather to understand their underlying logic and on that basis to discern carefully which parts of them might still be relevant. Part of this process includes taking account of New Testament cues where they are to be found. And in the case of these verses, there is a plausible case that the two principal New Testament passages outside of Romans that do appear to refer to same-sex relations are in fact deliberately evoking these Leviticus prohibitions and are therefore in a sense re-legislating them. In 1 Corinthians 6.9–10 Paul refers to those he calls *arsenokoitai* and *malakoi* as being among those who will not inherit the Kingdom of God, while in 1 Timothy 1.10 *arsenokoitai* are listed among those who display behaviour contrary to the sound teaching of the gospel.

Inevitably the Greek terms in these two texts have given rise to copious amounts of speculation. On the basis of later parallel usages in vice lists, some have claimed that *arsenokoitai* are those who commit some kind of sin of injustice associated with sex, while *malakoi* refers to male prostitutes or to men who have become feminized in some way, not necessarily through taking the passive role in homosexual sexual relations. Now such parallels and contextual points may have some purchase, but in the case of *arsenokoitai*, which literally means 'lying with a male', the strong probability is that Paul is coining a word on the basis of the Septuagint Greek translation of the original Hebrew of Leviticus. Similarly the 1 Timothy passage explicitly refers to the law as the context of the prohibitions, and there is a good case to be made that the list of the lawless is based loosely on the Ten Commandments, and therefore that it is a breach of the commandment against adultery which is being alluded to. In other words, in using this language Paul is restating the Leviticus case, which is in turn based on the claims in Genesis about sexuality in creation.

Some other parallels

The discussion of the biblical texts given here is exceptionally sketchy, as anyone remotely familiar with the literature will know. Moreover, it is one that for present purposes is reasonably content to acquiesce in relatively conventional readings of the texts.

But this is for a reason. The aim is not to provide a complete survey of the scholarship on biblical views of homosexuality, but rather to propose a strategy for reading the texts. What I am working towards is a claim that all the verses that refer to same-sex sexuality assume the Genesis patterning, that in creation sexuality is ordered to marital relationships between male and female, and that marital relationships are inseparable from an openness to procreation. In other words, their reasons for rejecting same-sex relationships are not based on any understanding of complementarity which is separable from the role of the two sexes in procreation. The importance of this is, of course, that it opens up the possibility that if we consider the eschatological significance of Christ for sexuality, different vistas may open up. As we have seen, if continuing procreation is no longer part of human fulfilment in the life to come, this cannot but affect our understanding of what sexuality can mean for those awaiting that fulfilment. And if we accept that sex even in a non-procreative context can be good, and that there is no final reason why all committed relationships should be intrinsically or deliberately open to procreation, we are opening the way to same-sex sexual relationships.

The most obvious response to this from the New Testament is that Paul appears explicitly to rule this out. Even if Romans 1 only refers to a breach of the creation good, as is required by the position in his argument, Paul gives no indication that he thinks that there is a wider theological context which would suddenly make same-sex relations morally acceptable. If 1 Corinthians 6 does indeed refer to those engaged in same-sex sexual behaviour, it makes clear the eschatological context according to which wrongdoers of those kinds will not inherit the Kingdom of God. And we might add in a number of verses that, while not explicitly referring to same-sex relations, might plausibly be thought to do so – notably those such as Ephesians 5.5 that refer to *porneia*, a catch-all word for sexual immorality often translated as 'fornication' – and moreover do so in an eschatological context. Paul's sexual ethics, and perhaps by extension that of the New Testament as a whole, could on this account be understood as an ethics of creation renewed. Moreover, given his context it could not possibly have been otherwise. Indeed, as Richard Hays remarks, '[if] Jesus or his followers had practised or countenanced homosexuality, it would have been profoundly scandalous within first-century Jewish culture'.[2]

But does the fact that it would have been impossible in the first century mean that it must also be impossible for us? This would not be the first time where something widely accepted by Christians now has been adopted in the face of biblical texts. One example of a practice that the New Testament did not reject out of hand, but that is universally condemned by Christians now, is slavery. 'Slaves, obey your earthly masters with fear and trembling, in singleness of heart, as you obey Christ' (Eph. 6.5). 'Slaves, obey your earthly masters in everything, not only while being watched and in order to please them, but wholeheartedly, fearing the Lord' (Col. 3.22). 'Let all those who are under the yoke of slavery regard their masters as worthy of all honour' (1 Tim. 6.1). Nineteenth-century slave-owners opposed to abolition had a wealth of texts on which they could instantly draw, and there is no evidence that the New Testament ever envisaged a future where slavery would not be a fact of life: humanized and made more decent, certainly ('Masters, treat your slaves justly and fairly' (Col. 4.1)), but never eliminated entirely.

Another obvious example is the role of women both in the Church and within marriage. As we saw in the previous chapter, Paul found weighty theological reasons to justify women being veiled while they prayed or prophesied, rooted in a hierarchy of being: 'a man ought not to have his head veiled, since he is the image and reflection of God; but woman is the reflection of man' (1 Cor. 11.7). He clearly found it intolerable that this symbolic order should be upset and reaches for every intellectual weapon he can find to make the point: doesn't 'nature itself' teach that it is degrading for a man to have long hair, but the glory of a woman to do so (1 Cor. 11.14–15)? In 1 Timothy we find women required

---

2 Richard B. Hays, *The Moral Vision of the New Testament: A Contemporary Introduction to New Testament Ethics*, Edinburgh: T & T Clark, 1997, p. 395.

to learn in silence in church in full submission and forbidden to teach or have authority over a man; and again we are given theological reasons ('Adam was formed first, then Eve; and Adam was not deceived, but the woman was deceived and became a transgressor' (1 Tim. 2.14)). Submission also applies within marriage: 'Wives, be subject to your husbands, as is fitting in the Lord' (Col. 3.18). And Ephesians supplies the theological rationale: 'the husband is the head of the wife just as Christ is the head of the church, the body of which he is the Saviour' (Eph. 5.23). The sheer number of references in the New Testament, the seriousness of the theological grounding that was given and the intensity with which Paul and those writing in his name clearly felt the issues, all indicate the depth of the problem for a constructive biblically informed theology of gender roles. Even verses such as Galatians 3.28 about all being one in Christ Jesus were evidently regarded as fully compatible with significant inequalities in practice.

Perhaps the most common response is one version or another of the claim that in these cases at least there is a trajectory in Scripture that indicates a direction of travel. In the case of slavery, even if New Testament writers never imagined a future without the practice, it could also be said that they never actively promote or teach it. Indeed the New Testament arguably does much to undermine the institution from within: Paul's letter to Philemon, pleading with the slave-owner that his slave is a brother in the Lord, provides the strongest possible theological case for regarding slaves and masters as equals; likewise Ephesians reminds masters that both slaves and masters have the same Master in heaven, with whom there is no partiality (Eph. 6.9). In the case of the role of women, there is the grounding principle of Galatians 3.28, together with the evident stress on reciprocity and mutual submission found in different ways in the household tables of the Epistles, and many other hints throughout the New Testament, some of which were alluded to in the last chapter in the brief discussion of the biblical basis for sexual equality; all of these point to the first signs of a breaking in of a different order. Again, in the case of remarriage after divorce, another issue often mentioned in this context, those arguing for the possibility of remarriage after divorce against Jesus' apparent rigorism, can appeal to the Matthean exception ('except on the ground of *porneia*' (Matt. 5.32; 19.9)) or the Pauline privilege ('if the unbelieving partner separates, let it be so' (1 Cor. 7.15)). In other words, in all these cases, Scripture itself provides a basis for rejecting, eliding or otherwise qualifying the seemingly plain teaching of Scripture, whereas in the case of same-sex relationships Scripture provides no basis for such a development.

But it is precisely this conclusion that it has been the burden of the first three chapters to contest. The implications for sexuality of Christ's coming are not drawn simply from an isolated verse about human beings being like angels in heaven, that as a result of the resurrection death shall be no more and so also birth and marriage shall be no more (Luke 20.35–36). Rather the whole eschatological and ascetic thrust of the New Testament is towards a vision of the resurrection life which, against the majority Jewish teaching of the time, is not a repristination of marriage and family life but a life beyond marriage, sex and family altogether. Jesus' own likely choice of celibacy, his radical redefinition of membership of his family ('Who is my mother, and who are my brothers?' (Matt. 12.48–50)), his call that one give up the most exigent of family responsibilities for the sake of following him ('Let the dead bury their own dead' (Matt. 8.21–22)) and his declaration that some have made themselves eunuchs for the sake of the Kingdom of heaven (Matt. 19.12), all point to this kind of conclusion. Likewise do Paul's own unmarried state, his wish that all be as he is (1 Cor. 7.7) and his reluctant acceptance that it is better to marry than to burn (1 Cor. 7.9). The overall New Testament emphasis that it is no longer human family lineage that matters, neither ancestry nor progeny, but incorporation in the body of Christ and sharing in the blood of Christ; its mysterious silence about the positive good of having children, as opposed to welcoming or disciplining those who happen to exist; and its endorsement of marriage and the family, but only as a second best to celibacy – all of these point to a profound reorientation of the creation goods of marriage and procreation. Marriage is second best, not because sex is bad, but because marriage and procreation are transitory, whereas celibacy points to the life immortal. In other words, there being no procreation in heaven is not an isolated and detachable theme in the New Testament but a central constituent of its entire theological vision.

When we add to this two further claims – first, that the initial reason given in Genesis and the only finally defensible reason for marriage being sexually differentiated is its aptitude for procreation, and therefore that there is theological space for eschatologically grounded covenant partnerships which need not be sexually differentiated because procreation will not feature in the resurrection life; and second, that in this life sex can be a good even when non-procreative – then we have the beginnings of a general case not only for non-procreative but still sexually active heterosexual covenant partnerships but also for same-sex relationships as well.

We can therefore be open to taking the criticism on the chin: even if there is no surface trajectory in the New Testament towards same-sex relationships, there are still a variety of reasons for finding such a rationale that arise from within the New Testament and that are in sympathy with its fundamental commitments.

Of course, it may be that we do not need to read the texts that purport to refer to same-sex behaviour so conventionally. I have deliberately acquiesced in relatively conservative readings, not because I necessarily finally endorse those readings, but because even if they are broadly correct they are not necessarily all that is to be said: we do not need to claim that the Bible was secretly pro-gay if only we could understand its context properly. It may well be that there is more to be uncovered than I have yet allowed. Maybe Paul had no notion of our modern understanding of sexual orientation and might have thought differently if he had? Maybe he assumed that most same-sex relationships were conducted by already married men who were behaving contrary to their own nature? Maybe he thought that homosexual adventures were conducted by heterosexuals bored with conventional sex? Maybe he assumed that sexual relations should always be between unequals, that they always symbolized and required a social hierarchy of superior and inferior which might be imperilled by same-sex relations? Or maybe he thought that sexual relations should always be between equals and that the kinds of homosexual relationship he was familiar with involved an unequal relationship that threatened this? Maybe he had never encountered consensual same-sex relationships committed to faithfulness and permanence? Maybe he had never had the kind of experience of life that would have allowed him to form any distinction between generalized sexual immorality and licentiousness on the one hand and stable, faithful same-sex partnerships on the other?

On all these and many other similar questions about the first-century context of the New Testament writings much has been said and no doubt much more could be said. I will limit myself to one observation here. Even if Paul was aware of consensual, committed same-sex partnerships from literature, philosophy or general observation of life, it is one thing to know about them in the abstract, another to know about them from close acquaintance and to begin to ponder and weigh their significance. And even if he had begun that process and had started to entertain strange thoughts about them – and there is no evidence at all to suggest this, we should be clear – the overwhelming social, religious, pragmatic and rhetorical pressures would have made it all but impossible for him to have written differently than he did. But the fact that it would have been impossible for him does not mean that it is necessarily impossible for us who live in the space shaped by the story of which he was the apostle.

Love and war

As it happens, there is another moral issue that involves reading the New Testament against its plain meaning, which is rarely invoked in this context. Defences of armed conflict have been offered in the Christian tradition ever since Augustine: the first Christians fought in 177, and there is some evidence that by 403 only Christians were allowed to fight in the imperial army. In the centuries since then, fighting has increasingly been thought to be compatible with the gospel, usually justified by moral theological appeal to the developing doctrine of just war.

On the face of it, this seems a flat contradiction of the teachings of the Prince of Peace, as generations of leisured cynics as well as principled pacifists have not been slow to mention. Opposition to war and military service in the early Church was sustained for many reasons, but there is little doubt that prime among them was that Christians thought that refusal to fight was required of them as part of their discipleship of Jesus. And it is hard to fault the thought. 'But I say to you, Do not resist an evildoer. But if anyone strikes you on the right cheek, turn the other also' (Matt. 5.39). 'You have heard that it was said, "You shall love your neighbour and hate your enemy." But I say to you, Love your enemies and pray for those who persecute you, so that you may be children of your Father in heaven' (Matt. 5.43–45). 'Beloved, never avenge yourselves, but leave room for the wrath of God; for it is written, "Vengeance is mine, I will repay, says the Lord"' (Rom. 12.19). Even though armed resistance to the Roman occupying forces was an option for Jesus' contemporaries, his refusal to interpret the Kingdom of God in similarly military terms indicates that the path of discipleship lay elsewhere.

Given the overwhelming New Testament evidence that suggested the irreconcilability of military service with the demands laid on the follower of Jesus, how did the Church come to endorse it? Augustine argued on the basis of the dual love command, the love that is the fulfilling of the law; Christian soldiers might fight so long as peace is the object of their desire, not war. This passing age is one in which evil has to be tolerated and war is waged as a necessity with the aim of peace. Subsequent analysis would provide more detail for the claim that war could be justified on the basis of love; for love of a weaker neighbour might require defending them against the injustice of a strong neighbour, even if love of the stronger neighbour also required that the resistance to them use only as much force as was necessary and no more. War, in other words, could be justified as a kind of concession to the time between the times, on the grounds that it was required by the love that is the fulfilment of the law.

I raise this not in order to pursue the moral issue of just war, but as a means of sharpening the question of the role of love in moral discernment. Why is it that war, and therefore who one may kill, can be widely justified in the Christian tradition by appeal to love, whereas same-sex relations, and therefore who one may love, cannot? The irony of not being able to appeal to love in order to justify love has not been lost on the many critics of current church teaching.

Against this charge, we do need to recognize that there are reasons for the reticence about simple appeals to love in moral theology, which deserve to be taken seriously. 'But I love her and she loves me,' says the middle-aged executive to his tearful wife as he drives off in the car with his secretary. Love is constantly in danger not of fulfilling the law, but of forgetting it; while the law frequently constrains our desires, it does so precisely because it maps out the shape of love. 'We know that the law is good', if one uses it in accordance with its proper nature (1 Tim. 1.8). The situationist programme in Protestant ethics, which gained much attention in the decades following the 1960s, was an effort to define love as the sole moral norm, and interpret all moral rules as rules of thumb that could be overridden if they conflicted with love; but it never ultimately commanded widespread allegiance, not least because it was never finally able to prevent itself from degenerating into a series of problematic utilitarianisms.[3]

Nevertheless, even if the law inescapably shows the way of love, love also shows the point of the law. And this presses a question to us. If prohibitions against same-sex relationships on the basis of biblical injunctions are to be sustained as part of Christian discipleship and are not to be viewed warily as the inscrutable commands of a distant deity, some effort has to be made to show what human good they serve. Why is *this* the way of love? What glimpses of human fulfilment does it point to? If perhaps it is for

---

3 Joseph Fletcher, *Situation Ethics: The New Morality*, London: SCM Press, 1966. Cf. Gene H. Outka and Paul Ramsey (eds), *Norm and Context in Christian Ethics* [1968], London: SCM Press, 1969, and Stanley Hauerwas, 'Situation Ethics, Moral Notions, and Moral Theology', in *Vision and Virtue: Essays in Christian Ethical Reflection* [1974], Notre Dame, IN: University of Notre Dame Press, 1981, pp. 11–29.

some wider good of society for which I as an individual may have to sacrifice myself, what is that wider good, and why does it demand this sacrifice? If it is for my good, what good might that be, or is it simply the satisfaction of knowing that I have lived in accordance with God's standards? And what purposes of the God of love might be behind God's standards? Even if it is dangerous to use the love command to short-circuit the detailed task of moral discernment, love is the sum of the law, and it does lay on us the constraint to begin to indicate what kind of human good is waited on by prohibiting same-sex relationships.

There are irreducible, surd elements in any interpretation of Scripture, texts that do not easily fit one's favoured view of the whole. The surd elements in the biblical interpretations of revisionist approaches to same-sex relationships have been widely rehearsed, even if they perhaps might be reframed somewhat, as I have tried to indicate in this chapter. But what these present thoughts on the dual love command also suggest is that there may be irreducible elements in more traditional approaches as well. Not only do they have to begin to show why this is the way of love, there are exceptionally problematic, not to say disastrous, pastoral and missiological consequences of conservative positions that may point us to other biblical themes that may not sit so well.

Finally, there is one more interesting feature about the debate between just war and pacifism in the churches. Although historically pacifist movements within Christianity have for understandable reasons often ended up forming separatist churches, this has not always been the case. At the present time most mainstream and historic churches have pacifist groupings within them and these are not generating calls for schism within the Church. The sociological reasons for this are no doubt worth exploring, but it does suggest that churches can hold together despite having members with disparate views about the interpretation of Scripture on some of the profoundest issues of Christian discipleship. To some extent they have been able to agree to disagree and yet hold together for common purpose in the gospel.

Is it possible to do the same thing in relation to same-sex relationships? In relation to reading the Bible, this would require one concession on the part of those who maintain a conservative position: namely a recognition that those who are exploring alternative positions should not be quickly condemned for simple disobedience to the plain meaning of Scripture, but may themselves also be seeking to interpret Scripture in a way more faithful to the trajectory of the texts than traditional readings have allowed. Theirs may or may not be the best interpretation, whatever that might mean, and it is certainly not the only one. But how might one go about deciding whether it is at least a legitimate one?

5

Same-Sex Marriage?

So far I have talked about marriage and covenant partnership as two separate vocations, the one grounded in creation and inseparable from procreation, the other grounded eschatologically and non-procreative in nature. The latter, let me say by way of reminder, could be heterosexual or homosexual. Moreover, covenant partnerships could be accompanied by children, which *ex hypothesi* could not be the fruit of their own sexual union, though they might be the result of adoption or fostering, or might be biologically related to just one of the couple for some other reason, for example that they were from a previous relationship.

The categories of marriage and covenant partnership that I have been employing so far have been resolutely theological in nature. In so far as this is an argument for covenant partnership, it is an argument for a new theological category, that is, a way for giving theological definition and intelligibility to certain kinds of relationships. This reflects a theme in much contemporary Christian ethics that the Church has to learn its own language first before it turns to address the world. If it fails to be shaped by its own story, it will inevitably be shaped by the stories of the world around it. If it is shaped by the stories of the world around it, it will in the end forget the one whose story it is called to tell.[1]

---

1 See, for example, the work of Stanley Hauerwas: accessible ways into his writings include *The Peaceable Kingdom: A Primer in Christian Ethics*, second edition, London: SCM Press, 2003, and *The Hauerwas Reader*, ed. John Berkman and Michael Cartwright, Durham, NC: Duke University Press, 2001.

However, if the first task of the Church is to learn what it is to be the Church, its second and corresponding task is to learn to relate its story to the world. It is one thing for the Church to become a *counter*-story, but if it is to be good news to the world it must also become a site for *en*counter.[2] What we now need to ask is how the new category of covenant partnership might map on to the categories of marriage and other legally recognized relationships that can be found in wider society. To attempt this in any systematic way would be a burden beyond endurance, in view of the variety of practice around the world: most countries only admit (traditional, heterosexual) marriage (thus also the UK until 2004), but some have marriage and same-sex civil partnerships (the UK from 2004 to 2013), some have equal marriage and same-sex civil partnerships (the UK from 2013 onwards), some have equal marriage and equal civil partnerships (the UK at some stage in the future?), and there are other further permutations. And in different countries there are different arrangements for the legal registration of these various relationships. In England, for example, the situation is complicated inasmuch as the Church of England is the established Church and its canon law is part of the law of the land; moreover, since Church of England parochial clergy are under a common law duty to marry any qualifying couple that lives within their parish, a change in the legal definition of marriage might potentially have very serious consequences in requiring clergy to marry same-sex couples against canon law.[3]

Because different jurisdictions have different laws relating to marriage and same-sex relationships, as well as different understandings of the relationship of Church and state, there cannot

---

2 As Bernd Wannenwetsch enquires of Stanley Hauerwas, 'must seeking the good of the city not also include the question of how the *counter*-mode can be perceived as a mode of *en*counter too?' (*Political Worship: Ethics for Christian Citizens*, tr. Margaret Kohl, Oxford: Oxford University Press, 2004, p. 246).

3 The Marriage (Same Sex Couples) Act 2013 addresses this by providing a 'quadruple lock' intended to safeguard clergy in the Church of England and the Church of Wales from being required to conduct a same-sex marriage without a further formal change in the law.

be a single prescription for how this might work out in practice. Indeed not only are there wide legal variations across the globe relating to same-sex relationships, ranging from hanging or stoning at the one extreme to public celebration of gay marriage at the other, there are also different legal provisions for marriage, ranging from those that adhere quite closely to a traditional Christian understanding of marriage, on the one hand, to those that permit polygamy or have exacting requirements about exogamy on the other. Even in England, where historically the legal requirements for a valid marriage were those established in the canon law of the Church of England, there were moves away from the Church's historic understanding of marriage long before the legalization of equal marriage, not least in the changes made to the Table of Kindred and Affinity inaugurated by the Deceased Wife's Sister's Marriage Act of 1907.

We need to tread carefully, therefore. The changes that are happening at a pace – not least in the UK – call for considerable discernment, and the discussion here will be particularly tentative. In this chapter, I will be laying out some possibilities rather than firmly arguing for any one of them.

Covenant partnership as civil partnership

One option would be to correlate covenant partnership and civil partnership. Because the direction of the argument has been to base covenant partnerships not in creation but in the eschatological orientation made possible with the coming of Christ, there is a strong prima facie case for considering whether that contrast might take advantage of an existing legal distinction between marriage and civil partnership. In Britain now, for example, civil partnerships can be contracted between two persons of the same sex, giving them largely identical rights and responsibilities to those that they would gain in marriage, but with some differences, notably in the grounds for dissolution, which do not include adultery or non-consummation. It might fit quite neatly if in the churches' teaching and practice (traditional, opposite-sex) marriage continued to be celebrated as marriage, but civil partnerships were opened up as a possible legal route for same-sex relationships and indeed for heterosexual covenant partnerships. Those who felt called to covenant partnership would then have a civil ceremony which gave them the legal status of civil partnership, but would have a liturgical blessing in church to covenant partnership; whether that civil partnership might also be performed in church as a unified ceremony at once legal and ecclesiastical, so that clergy could be registrars for civil partnership, would be a matter for further determination.

The attraction of this route is that it brings out very clearly the force of the underlying theological distinction between marriage and covenant partnership. It would repeat firmly in the public realm the idea that marriage in creation is sexually differentiated because of its openness to procreation. And it would make use of a legal category that might in fact do all that the churches ask of it, with the exception that civil partnership would need to be extended to heterosexual relationships, since covenant partnership can be homosexual or heterosexual. Indeed, precisely because civil partnerships do not assume a sexual relationship (non-consummation is not a legal ground for dissolution), it would emphasize that the primary issue is the nature of the relationship, not whether it is sexually expressed.

However, there are also potentially several problems with it. Let us note first an issue that was left slightly hanging from the discussion in Chapter 2. There I observed that deliberately childless marriages have been formally endorsed by the Church of England as marriages for the better part of a century, despite their lack of rationale in terms of a formal theology of creation which makes procreation an inseparable part of the good of marriage. Whether we endorse calling them marriage or not, that language has become so entrenched in Anglican and Protestant churches that the suggestion that deliberately childless marriages constitute a failure to understand the nature of marriage is widely met with incredulity. Of course the churches could seek to restore the historic Christian teaching and practice, and I argued for this in the earlier discussion. But realistically it remains probable that most heterosexual couples intending not to have children would still opt for marriage: in practice if covenant partnership were paired with civil partnership, it would principally be same-sex relationships that were involved, distorting the theological point.

Second, we need to think through the implications of what initially appears as a series of practical problems. What if a heterosexual couple who had embarked on a covenant partnership then decided that they wanted to have children? Or if they had embarked on marriage and then had decided they wished to be childless? In either case, would the change in the status of their relationship need to be formally recognized and, if so, how? These present as practical or legal problems, but they point to an interconnection between marriage and covenant partnership, one that is reinforced when we also recall from our earlier discussion that there are ways in which the category of covenant partnerships, characterized by non-procreative fruitfulness, could illuminate and confer a sense of fulfilment on marriages that are contingently childless because of age or infertility. Indeed, once the category is available it is moot whether couples embarking on marriage knowing that they will not be able to have children are better regarded as entering into marriage or covenant partnership. That illumination of the one relationship by the other could only occur if there was some kind of inward relationship between them.

The third problem is the one that will most readily occur to most people, namely that marriage and civil partnership are widely perceived as being unequal. And this for a variety of reasons. The language of 'civil partnership' itself feels bureaucratic and distancing. Moreover, because the ceremony only requires the signing of a legal document before witnesses, and does not obligate the couple expressly to promise that they will love, comfort, honour, protect and be faithful to the other as long as they both shall live, it can seem a bloodless and romance-free way of distributing property rights that says little about the mutuality, heartfeltness and lifelong commitment that the idea of marriage is evidently still thought to convey. Perhaps most importantly of all, civil partnership has been felt to be yet another way of ensuring that gay people are excluded from the full social recognition that is conferred by marriage. Certainly there was early resistance to the idea of same-sex marriage by many LGBT activists and organizations who had for long-standing reasons been suspicious of the repressive and patriarchal nature of traditional marriage, and had found gay, lesbian and other non-heteronormative identities personally liberating and an attractive form of social radicalism. As a result, for a good number of same-sex couples the possibility of civil partnership therefore presented itself as a way of publicly expressing love and permanence of relationship, obtaining recognition (not least by family members), and acquiring legal benefits, all without the baggage of traditional marriage. But for all this, despite the high take-up, civil partnership has still been unable entirely to shake off the sense of being fundamentally second class, a junior partner to marriage.

The position set out in this book also rejects the idea that covenant partnerships should be regarded as second best to marriage, grudgingly tolerated as a pragmatic accommodation or bolted on as an outhouse to the main building. However, it is of the utmost importance that we be clear why this should be so. The present argument does not involve an appeal to 'equal marriage' in an abstract liberal egalitarian sense that denies the significance of sexual difference. It does not claim that one's biological sex no longer matters and therefore that it makes no difference whether marriage is between partners of the same sex or partners of different sexes. On the contrary, marriages between partners of different sexes are significant because they are capable in principle of producing children, the fact to which the existence of contraception bears witness; by contrast, same-sex relationships can only be procreative indirectly, either through the involvement of a third party or through the application of technologies as yet unknown. Rather, the reason for seeing covenant partnerships and marriages as equal is that theologically they are both vocations. Just as marriage is one vocation, and celibacy a second, so covenant partnership is a third. To each is given a gift and, exactly because it is a gift that each is given, there is no ground for boasting or for regarding one as better than another.

Theologically therefore there is no reason for regarding marriage as of any different value from covenant partnership. If civil partnership were the way in which covenant partnerships were given legal recognition, there would be no theological reason for regarding civil partnership as inferior to marriage. For this reason, there would be a particular attractiveness in a situation in which civil partnership was the means by which Christians might translate publicly for legal purposes their own commitment to covenant partnership.

But churches do not exist in spaces insulated from their surrounding cultures. This is true for all churches at all times, but it is of especial significance for those churches that prize closeness to their host societies rather than distance from them and that do not set up onerous partitions between membership and non-membership. For them the proper inclusion of marriage discipline within church discipline is in tension with their desire, or indeed legal obligation, to offer marriage to all eligible couples who ask. If it were the case that civil partnerships came to be irretrievably regarded as clearly inferior, that in itself might be a reason for letting the legal recognition of covenant partnerships take the form of marriage, since the public perception of inferiority would give the lie to their theological standing. Certainly theologically, covenant partnerships are a different calling from marriage and therefore should not be regarded or symbolized as being second in rank to it, but as unqualifiedly and unapologetically equal. Their existence would not depend on pastoral concession or missiological pragmatism; they would stand not on any external worldly acknowledgement or legal recognition, but on Christ. But if covenant partnerships were publicly perceived to be second class because of their association with civil partnerships, it might be better – and this would be a prudential pastoral and missiological judgement, based on a balancing of the different factors – for them to be correlated to marriage in order that their equal status in Christ not be lost in translation.

For all these reasons, we need to reckon with the possibility of the legal recognition of covenant partnerships through marriage.

Covenant partnership as marriage

One way of doing this might be to regard covenant partnerships simply as marriage, *tout court*. The Church might choose to bless the civil marriages of same-sex couples while continuing to conduct weddings of heterosexual couples; or, more desirably, apply for legal restrictions to be removed so that it could conduct marriages of all couples regardless of their gender make-up. Liturgies would have to be adapted by adopting inclusive or 'he/she' language, and ever more brackets of optionality would have to be inserted around references to the birth of children; and so on. The marriage ministry of the Church would proceed more or less as before, the only difference being that some heterosexual couples would choose not to have children (a nicety which would be noticed by scarcely anyone), and some weddings would be of gay or lesbian couples (something that would be noticed by everyone initially, until they had settled down and got used to it).

This would have the advantage of ease, and no doubt for church managers this would make it the most attractive option. But it would also face severe problems. It would lend itself too easily to the denial of the significance of sexual difference, with consequences not only for our understanding of ourselves as occupying a place on the spectrum of sexual differentiation, but also for our understanding of sexual relations: sex would easily become whatever we choose to make it mean, its procreative capacity becoming a contingent feature of it. (Would sexual relations be intrinsic to marriage? And if not, would the liturgy still wish to refer to the delight and tenderness of sexual union?) It would be in danger of losing the theological narrative that gives shape to Christian convictions: timeless claims about human beings, too easily detached from their mooring in Christ both as the one through whom creation came to be and the one in whom creation has its fulfilment, would readily replace the theological specificity for which I have argued throughout this book. (Would the liturgy refer to marriage as a gift of God in creation? And how would it expound this? Or would it elide the question altogether?) And so the Church's witness on marriage might find itself yielding to secular trends, capitulating to Enlightenment claims about equal individual contractors replacing Christian claims about creation, covenant and calling. It might acquiesce in the basic redefinition of marriage implied by the notion of equal marriage, but at considerable theological loss. And finally, because covenant partnership would have no visible place in the Church's ministry, it might close the door on the notion of covenant partnership showing us anything different about the possibilities for human relationship; by locking them all up under the category of marriage, it would inevitably act as a force for normalisation and conventionality. Same-sex marriage on the liberal egalitarian model, whereby all difference is erased, might end up ironically being the most conservative of options, and the particular gifts that lesbians, gays, transsexuals and intersex people, as well as heterosexual couples wishing to explore forms of non-procreative vocation, might bring to the Church and to wider society would be suffocated in a smog of conformity.

Marriage as covenant partnership

Both alternatives I have considered so far, covenant partnership as civil partnership and covenant partnership as marriage, have presumed that our theological understanding of marriage remains untouched. Although I have resisted so far seeing marriage as anything other than a creation ordinance, another alternative would be to see marriage itself as changed theologically by the coming of Christ. Might it be that after the birth of Christ covenant partnership is the deeper and more embracing category, with procreative marriage now being the special case? Rather than placing them as two different vocations side by side, might in fact marriage be subsumed under covenant partnership, such that procreation was a contingent result of marriage? All covenant partnerships would be characterized by faithfulness, permanence and fruitfulness, but in some cases that fruitfulness would take the specific form of children from within the couple's sexual relationship, in other cases it would take the form of any number of kinds of works of charity, including not least adoption and fostering. This would bring out the theological truth, and not just the moral exhortation, in Gregory of Nyssa's counsel that once children have left home and a couple's immediate responsibilities to them have died down, the couple should devote themselves to works for the poor.

There are many attractions to this approach. It would give a unified theological account of marriage and covenant partnership, bringing out the subterranean connections between the two, and also showing how a creation ordinance is taken up and fulfilled eschatologically without losing its grounding in creation. It would make clear that marriages are always between equals: same-sex covenant partnerships cannot be understood as unions hierarchically ordered by gender and so the claim that marriage itself would necessarily be between equals would be fundamentally confirmed. It would revivify the Christian understanding that marriages are *always* for something beyond themselves, not just for the personal fulfilment of the couple. Just as we saw that covenant partnerships must always be characterized by fruitfulness in doing the works of the Lord so as to avoid the dangers of an *égoisme à deux*, so we would understand that procreative marriages are also always oriented to procreation as a species of fruitfulness and therefore oriented beyond themselves. Marriages too carry the danger of forming introverted happy families, and need to be reminded that children are a good in themselves while also pointing beyond themselves, inasmuch as they are tokens of the hospitality and openness to the other that all marriages are called to. The witness of the Christian Church in marriage would then clearly be demarcated not as a paean to the nuclear family, let alone to patriarchal models of marriage, but rather to the avoidance of self-centred and consumerist models of marriage and family. Marriage enriches society and strengthens community, yet it does so not by raising new generations of consumers, but by nurturing people who are capable of love.

To abandon the *language* of 'marriage' in favour of the language of 'covenant partnership' or something similar would be a step only the bravest of ecclesiastical pioneers could contemplate. And it would be unnecessary. For in pointing marriage to its own eschatological

orientation it would be reworking marriage from within and showing that it itself had become something new in Christ. Certainly, the
liturgy of marriage would need to be very substantially rethought,
yet it would do so in a way that was not a haphazard meddling with
the traditional marriage service to accommodate new demands, but
a unified and integrated theological whole.

It is important to appreciate how significant a move this would
be. Although I have presented 'marriage as covenant partnership'
as the third of a series of practical and liturgical alternatives, it
would constitute a very significant theological change. It would
indicate that marriage has been decisively affected by the new
eschatological context in Christ, that the third vocation has in
fact reworked the nature of marriage itself. Although it would
not change one of the fundamental contentions of this book, that
the coming of Christ has made an essential change to the nature
of human sexuality, it would require a reworking, in the light of
the new eschatological reality, of some of the material in earlier
chapters on marriage as a creation ordinance. And, practically,
for a variety of reasons it is likely that churches would need to
explore whether it was possible to preserve a separate liturgy for
'traditional' marriage, that is, marriage as understood in terms of
creation norms.

Conclusion

This chapter has been left deliberately tentative, partly because
there are so many contexts in which the Church's teaching on
marriage and sexuality has to be worked out, and partly because
even within the context of Britain, and more specifically England,
there are many imponderables to be weighed. These three routes –
covenant partnership as civil partnership, covenant partnership as
marriage, and marriage as covenant partnership – are presented as
options, each of which would require further elaboration beyond
the initial sketches outlined here. There are no doubt further alternatives as well. But however the path from theological reflection to
liturgical, pastoral and legal practice is traced, the crucial question

must always be whether the Church's practice in relation to marriage and sexuality is finally driven by its own deepest commitments, or by accommodation to the prevailing culture in which it is immersed. This brings us to the question of discernment, which is taken up in the final chapter.

6

Conclusion

The churches are still reeling from the changes in sexual mores that emerged across Western societies in the second half of the twentieth century. And it is not surprising: the extent of the transformation that we have come to know as the sexual revolution is genuinely remarkable and in some ways unprecedented in human history. The task of reorienting themselves to radically changed circumstances is not one that comes to the churches quickly, and will continue to demand of them exceptional powers of discernment as they seek to witness to the gospel as good news for each successive generation.

Up until the 1950s in Britain – and broadly similar stories can be told of many Western countries – the dominant code of sexual ethics was one that was recognizably Christian in nature. The culture normalized marriage and the traditional two-parent family. Sex was meant to be kept within the bounds of marriage and sexual restraint was enforced – especially by women and even within marriage – for fear of pregnancy. Divorce was difficult, socially unacceptable, and expensive. Sex before marriage was far from unknown (just before the Second World War 30 percent of mothers were reported to have been pregnant on getting married), but it was probably mainly confined to those who were expecting to get married. Much effort was put into preservation of the façade of respectability: marriage was expected to follow on the discovery of pregnancy (and sometimes was only allowed if pregnancy was confirmed), children would be quietly adopted by relatives within the family if needed to preserve decorum, and the imperatives of the gendered family order would be observed. This necessarily required the externalizing and stigmatizing of individuals who represented the failure of the dominant order:

single mothers, illegitimate children and homosexuals among them. Marriage therefore was at the heart of a patriarchal order, carrying with it a gendered division of labour, one whose pressures (not least of repeated and potentially dangerous pregnancy) bore particularly hard on women, but also one that gave women social standing and ensured their safety from the inevitable poverty that accompanied single motherhood.

Whatever particular pastoral problems the churches may have had to deal with, it was nevertheless a mainly coherent and broadly Christian whole, one in which they could feel at home. Deviations from received norms could be coded as the result of moral lapse, not as a threat to the Christian order as a whole. The connection between Christianity and social order, to allude to the title of Archbishop William Temple's 1942 book that was to be enormously influential on the shape of the post-war social settlement, was one that could be readily made and widely recognized. The task of Christian social ethics was one of reminding the broader culture of its own best commitments and spelling out the practical principles that would mediate between Christian ideals and empirical reality. And until the 1950s those principles could reasonably be thought to govern the conduct of marriage and family life as well as the workings of the economy and the welfare state, which had been Temple's more immediate concern.

Since then, it is fair to say that, amid the changes that have happened, within mainstream society almost every principal strand of traditional Christian teaching on sexuality and marriage has unravelled, in terms both of the dominant social norms and the lived reality. Sex is no longer confined to marriage, as can be seen in the widespread culture of casual non-marital and pre-marital sex and the statistics on cohabitation rates – though the norm of fidelity within marriage remains largely preserved. Parenting is no longer largely related to marriage, as attested by the rise of non-married parents and of single parents (usually mothers and usually as a result of relationship breakdown). Sex is no longer inextricably linked to procreation, as a result of the availability of safe and effective contraception on the one hand, and the rise of IVF and a range of assisted reproduction techniques on the other. The gender order has shifted, the segregated division of labour between paid work and the domestic economy being replaced by a more symmetrical balance of gender power. Family patterns have changed, with smaller families, shorter periods devoted to childbirth and more time given to child-rearing, and a rise in cohabitation and non-traditional family forms. Attitudes to the marginalized other have changed; instead of being ignored and then highlighted for their difference, gays and lesbians have become socially normalized, while the heteronormativity that generated their outsider status is itself being eroded. The willingness of individuals to avow publicly their sexuality and sexual activity has also risen, as has the fascination with previously marginalized forms of sexual behaviour: E. L. James's *Fifty Shades of Grey*, which features multiple scenes of sadomasochistic, bondage/submission practices, became on publication the fastest-selling paperback of all time. Across the entire population, attitudes of willingness to live with difference and of personal non-judgementalism have replaced habits of suspiciousness towards deviance, while moralizing discourse has given way to pragmatic judgements of trial and error about workable relationships – though interestingly the assumption that marriage is intended to be for life remains largely intact.

The reasons for these changes are complex and various. One significant material factor was unquestionably the arrival of the contraceptive pill. For the first time women, who had always of necessity been the guardians of the nation's sexual morals, could take control of their own fertility. The rising sense that women could take charge of their own destiny generated a sense of freedom of choice that was decisive for the changes that were to come. Ideologically the changes in attitudes to sexual mores away from the legal enforcement of dominant norms to a principled separation of the private from the public was emblematized in the pioneering work of the Wolfenden Report of 1957, recommending the decriminalization of consensual homosexual behaviour. Economically the rise of industrial but more especially post-industrial capitalism, together with the experience of the pluralization of the life-worlds within which people have to choose job and lifestyle options, and the gradual distancing from traditional social norms and practices – all of these and many other factors have created the sense that in post-traditional societies people have to negotiate for themselves a basis for personal identity and for life values that can no longer be taken for granted or received from recognized sources of authority.

It is wholly unsurprising that the churches have found all of this exceptionally unsettling. From time immemorial they had presided over a society in which they were responsible for articulating and enforcing a series of shared norms that were broadly consonant with Christian teaching, even if these were often adhered to for pragmatic reasons. Sharing moral authority with succeeding older generations who were responsible for cultural reproduction, their place in society was assured. It was quite understandable therefore that when the ground started moving beneath their feet, they would be most conscious not of positive aspects of the changes, but of the damage that was being caused. The rise in divorce, promiscuity, sexually transmitted diseases, abortion, child abuse, pornography and the general sexualization of culture, were all lumped together with the growing prominence of sexual minorities as evidence of an increasingly individualist, selfish and amoral society.

Correspondingly, it has been extremely difficult for the churches to acknowledge that in relation to sexual mores they have been flailing and unsure how to respond now for two generations. They have constantly been on the defensive, continually retrenching in reaction to pastoral pressure with regard to divorce and remarriage, cohabitation, premarital sex, abortion, same-sex relationships, and much else. To a significant extent many mainline churches have been unable to hold discipline even within their congregations beyond sustaining a general level of social respectability; and responses to legislative change, not least by the Church of England in relation to civil partnerships and equal marriage, have been perceived by many as flat-footed and mean-minded. In consequence, in the United Kingdom at least, the churches have to a significant extent lost their public moral authority on matters of sexuality and gender – by contrast, their ability to voice the conscience of the nation on matters of economics, poverty and welfare is striking. Perhaps above all, they have found it difficult to accept that the current situation is not a temporary aberration and that all probable forecasts suggest that things are not likely to change soon.

Of course, no one can predict the future. Many of the most significant geopolitical events of the last few decades were not widely predicted: the rise of Islam as a major political force, the fall of Communism, the atrocities of 9/11, the 2008 financial crisis. But there is no current sign of a major, politically cohesive internal reaction within Britain to the sexual revolution, the Coalition for Marriage notwithstanding. Although such a reaction certainly can be found in the global South – hence the travails of the Anglican Communion – the only prominent movement that widely impinges on domestic British sensibilities is that of politicized Islam. But one remarkable feature of the public reaction to Islamism is how little appetite there has been to engage with Islam's views on sex, gender and marriage. For all the problems that the revolution in sexual attitudes and behaviours has bequeathed, there is no evident desire to return to the previous order or anything like it. The predominant cultural mood continues to be one of liberation from the past, a tale incessantly repeated in a profusion of agony columns, TV soaps and dramas, novels and films. From the point of view of the babyboomers, the world we have lost felt like one of 'petty hypocrisies and restrictions, of constraints and restraints, of tradition and hierarchy that was a long time dying'.[1] And it is one that few are seeking to resuscitate.

All of this calls for a major reimagination of the churches' relations to the culture, one that no longer secretly draws sustenance from clinging to past settlements and that harbours no surreptitious hopes for returning to them. Such reimagination emphatically does not mean endorsement of current trends. On the contrary, it requires working out of the Church's own deepest and best understanding of its own resources, recognizing that its own part-marginality affords it the opportunity to step back and think creatively about how it is to engage. But equally, nor does

---

1 Jeffrey Weeks, *The World We Have Won*, Abingdon: Routledge, 2007, p. 58.

reimagination mean the easy alternative of a reactionary response that condemns the entire sexual revolution out of hand and presumptively convicts any defence of, say, same-sex relationships as a form of collaborationist betrayal. If the churches are to be heralds of good news in a changed world, their tone cannot be one of increasingly shrill and bitter denunciation.

The question is rather one of discernment, interrogating the times to see what is of value in them. This is a task required of us not by importing an implicit liberal progressivism, but by a theological understanding of history. It is of course easy for those who favour developments towards gender equality and sexual inclusion to read the history of the last few centuries as a story of incremental progress, of the triumph of the forces of light over against conservatism and the forces of darkness. But theologically we should be suspicious of grand narratives of history as inevitable if uneven progress. Not only do they lend themselves too uncritically towards conceits of Western exceptionalism and superiority to the non-Western other, habits of mind that engender understandable anxieties around the world about a new liberal imperialism. They also forget the theological truth that since the coming of Christ and the giving of the Holy Spirit no new events have happened that are decisive for human salvation. We live in a time between the times, a period within which all times are equidistant from God: the modern Western world is not necessarily nearer to God – nor, we should make clear against conservative predilections for declinist nostalgia, necessarily any further from God – than any other period of history.

The task of discernment is exceptionally complex. On the one hand, it requires an unflinchingly disabused awareness of the casualties of the sexual revolution, of the social consequences of marriage breakdown, of the effects – especially but not only on women – of an increasingly porn-drenched imagination, of the fall-out of the casualization of sex. On the other, it compels an appreciation of the undisputed gains of the past century: the changed status of women and the increased recognition of equality within marriage, the growing acknowledgement of rape and domestic violence, the rise in awareness of child abuse, and so on; in passing, we should not fail to note that the norm of fidelity within marriage and the presumption that marriage is to be for life are still widely endorsed. We also need to think through how sources of moral authority and the significance of that authority for people has changed. With the decline of traditional authority, people are forced on their own resources and find themselves having to negotiate lives in fluid circumstances over which they have varying degrees of control. This is not remotely the same as a dogmatic selfish individualism, but is more an effort to ensure one's emotional survival and retain a degree of personal integrity in the context of a realistic sense of what is pragmatically possible. And part of this is looking for guidance and reassurance from sources of authority that make sense to them, not those that lay oppressive burdens of moral rectitude, but those that manage to evoke in people some sense of personal meaningfulness and hope of a way forward.

It is too early to say what all this might mean for the churches' moral language and pastoral style. However, we might make a start by pondering observations such as the following: people will be drawn to the good by beauty rather than forced to it by the law; romantic and erotic desire point us towards God rather than away from God; it is better to make goodness possible rather than condemn where it is absent; marriages and committed relationships exist for goods beyond themselves, not just for the mutual satisfaction of the partners; and so on.

What the churches may wish to say about same-sex relationships is therefore just one part of a much wider set of engagements. Of course, rethinking what they say on this subject always runs the danger of being conformed to the reigning secular logics of our day. The call to reimagine the churches' engagement with the culture may never be identified with a surreptitious plea to accede to its demands: the Church only has one Lord and one Word of God, which it has to hear and which it has to trust and obey in life and death. But equally in the tasks of moral discernment to which we are called in our time and place, we are also required to test the spirits, to see which are of God. And that in turn requires an openness to being transformed, to the renewing of our minds as we present ourselves as offerings to God, members together of the body of Christ.

Futher Reading

I have kept the text deliberately light on footnotes and scholarly engagements in an effort to keep the line of the argument clearer and more accessible. As a way of making partial amends for this, here is an annotated list of some of the books I have engaged with and been influenced by.

On the Bible, William Loader, *The New Testament on Sexuality* (Grand Rapids, MI: Eerdmans, 2012), is a major recent overview. It is the last in a five-volume series on attitudes towards sexuality in early Judaism and Christianity; his findings are summarized for non-specialist readers in *Making Sense of Sex: Attitudes towards Sexuality in Early Jewish and Christian Literature* (Grand Rapids, MI: Eerdmans, 2013). Robert A. J. Gagnon, *The Bible and Homosexual Practice: Texts and Hermeneutics* (Nashville, TN: Abingdon Press, 2001), is the most comprehensive conservative reading; Gagnon also maintains a website with updates and further discussion at http://www.robgagnon.net/. Stephen D. Moore, *God's Beauty Parlor and Other Queer Spaces in and around the Bible* (Stanford: Stanford University Press, 2001) and Dale B. Martin, *Sex and the Single Savior: Gender and Sexuality in Biblical Interpretation* (Louisville, KY: Westminster John Knox Press, 2006), are examples of queer/radical readings. For an understanding of marriage and celibacy in the New Testament that might lead to different conclusions than those presented here, see Stephen C. Barton, *Discipleship and Family Ties in Mark and Matthew* (Cambridge: Cambridge University Press, 1994).

The theologians in the tradition who have most emphasized the significance of the advent of Christ for marriage and sexuality are

Augustine of Hippo and Karl Barth. Augustine's principal writings on sexuality are gathered in Elizabeth A. Clark (ed.), *St. Augustine on Marriage and Sexuality* (Washington, DC: Catholic University of America Press, 1996); for commentary, see also Paul Ramsey, 'Sexuality in the History of Redemption', *Journal of Religious Ethics* 16 (1988), pp. 56–86. A starting point for Barth's ethics of marriage and sexuality is *Church Dogmatics*, III.4: *The Doctrine of Creation* [1951], trans. A. T. MacKay et al. (Edinburgh: T & T Clark, 1961), pp. 116–240. For John Paul II's 'theology of the body', see *Man and Woman He Created Them: A Theology of the Body*, trans. Michael Waldstein (Boston, MA: Pauline Books and Media, 2006). An excellent overview of the theological tradition on sexual differentiation is found in Christopher Chenault Roberts, *Creation and Covenant: The Significance of Sexual Difference in the Moral Theology of Marriage* (New York: Continuum, 1997).

For histories of marriage and sexuality in the Christian tradition, see Peter Brown's unsurpassed and perhaps unsurpassable account of attitudes in the patristic period in *The Body and Society: Men, Women and Sexual Renunciation in Early Christianity* (New York: Columbia University Press, 1998) and John Witte Jr's excellent history of the theological and legal tradition, *From Sacrament to Contract: Marriage, Religion and Law in the Western Tradition* (Louisville, KY: Westminster John Knox Press, 1997).

Among the many recent writings, Rowan Williams, 'The Body's Grace' [1989] (available online and reprinted in many places), is described in the Eugene Rogers reader listed below as 'the best 10 pages written about sexuality in the twentieth century'. Michael Vasey, *Strangers and Friends: A New Exploration of Homosexuality and the Bible* (London: Hodder & Stoughton, 1995), Elizabeth Stuart, *Just Good Friends: Towards a Lesbian and Gay Theology of Relationships* (London: Cassell, 1995) and Timothy Bradshaw (ed.), *The Way Forward? Christian Voices on Homosexuality and the Church* (London: SCM Press, 2003) are three British discussions from the 1990s which have plenty of insight. Eugene F. Rogers Jr, *Sexuality and the Christian Body* (Oxford: Blackwell, 1999), is a defence of same-sex marriage with many brilliant emphases, including on marriage as an ascetic practice by which God takes up sexuality into God's own life. Jo Ind, *Memories of Bliss: God, Sex and Us* (London: SCM Press, 2003), is a gem of a book that explores the personal meanings of sexuality. Helen Savage's PhD thesis, 'Changing Sex? Transsexuality and Christian Theology' (Durham University, 2006, available online at http://library.dur.ac.uk; and forthcoming as a book), is a fine use of 'ordinary theology' methodology to analyse the experience of transsexuals. Gerard Loughlin (ed.), *Queer Theology: Rethinking the Western Body* (Malden, MA: Blackwell, 2007), is a wide-ranging collection of essays relating queer theory and Christian theology. Susannah Cornwall, *Sex and Uncertainty in the Body of Christ: Intersex Conditions and Christian Theology* (London: Equinox, 2010), investigates questions of the body and sexuality in relation to intersex. Jeffrey John, *Permanent, Faithful, Stable: Christian Same-Sex Marriage* [1993], new edition (London: Darton, Longman and Todd, 2012), provides a brief, accessible defence of same-sex marriage. Sarah Coakley, *God, Sexuality and the Self: An Essay 'On the Trinity'* (Cambridge: Cambridge University Press, 2013), integrates gender theory, spirituality and Trinitarian theology.

For two evangelical autobiographical perspectives, see Wesley Hill, *Washed and Waiting: Reflections on Christian Faithfulness and Homosexuality* (Grand Rapids, MI: Zondervan, 2010) and Graham Ingram, *Out of the Shadows* (Hertford: Church Home Group Resources, 2008).

Useful readers include Adrian Thatcher and Elizabeth Stuart (eds), *Christian Perspectives on Sexuality and Gender* (Leominster: Gracewing, 1996) and Eugene F. Rogers Jr (ed.), *Theology and Sexuality: Classic and Contemporary Readings* (Oxford: Blackwell, 2002). Adrian Thatcher, *God, Sex and Gender: An Introduction* (Oxford: Wiley-Blackwell, 2011) and Susannah Cornwall, *Theology and Sexuality* (London: SCM Press, 2013) are recent introductions.

Accounts of the significance of the sexual revolution include Jeffrey Weeks, *The World We Have Won: The Remaking of Erotic and Intimate Life* (Abingdon: Routledge, 2007) and Anthony

Giddens, *The Transformation of Intimacy: Sexuality, Love and Eroticism in Modern Societies* (Cambridge: Polity Press, 1992). Behind much recent writing on sexuality and gender are, unavoidably, the writings of Michel Foucault (see for example his first volume of *The History of Sexuality* [1976], trans. Robert Hurley (London: Allen Lane, 1979)) and Judith Butler (see for example *Gender Trouble: Feminism and the Subversion of Identity* (New York: Routledge, 1990)).

For specifically Anglican dimensions, Oliver O'Donovan, *Church in Crisis: The Gay Controversy and the Anglican Communion* (Eugene, OR: Wipf and Stock, 2008) (published in the UK as *A Conversation Waiting to Begin: The Churches and the Gay Controversy* (London: SCM Press, 2009)), is a characteristically shrewd account of the way ecclesial conversations should be conducted. The multi-authored 'Same-Sex Relationships and the Nature of Marriage: A Theological Colloquy' (published in *The Anglican Theological Review* 93:1 (2011)) contains a record of a recent round of theological deliberations in The Episcopal Church, USA. Timothy Willem Jones, *Sexual Politics in the Church of England, 1857–1957* (Oxford: Oxford University Press, 2013) gives a history of developments in the Church of England, while Miranda K. Hassett, *Anglican Communion in Crisis: How Episcopal Dissidents and Their African Allies Are Reshaping Anglicanism* (Princeton, NJ: Princeton University Press, 2007) and William L. Sachs, *Homosexuality and the Crisis of Anglicanism* (Cambridge: Cambridge University Press, 2009)' address the crisis in the global Anglican Communion. Mark Vasey-Saunders's PhD dissertation, 'The Problem of English Evangelicals and Homosexuality: A Girardian Study of Popular Evangelical Writings on Homosexuality 1960–2010' (Durham University, 2012, available online at http://library.dur.ac.uk; and forthcoming as a book), provides an intriguing account of the causes of English evangelical anxieties about homosexuality.

Among the many websites with up-to-date relevant material, those of Thinking Anglicans (www.thinkinganglicans.org.uk/, liberal Anglican) and Fulcrum (www.fulcrum-anglican.org.uk/, moderate evangelical) are particularly valuable.

Index of Bible References

Index of Names and Subjects

CPSIA information can be obtained at www.ICGtesting.com
Printed in the USA
LVOW09s2243031114

411895LV00013B/343/P